Contents

Monolingualism and Bilingualism

Lessons from Canada and Spain

Edited by
Sue Wright

MULTILINGUAL MATTERS LTD
Clevedon • Philadelphia • Adelaide

Library of Congress Cataloging in Publication Data

Monolingualism and Bilingualism: Lessons from Canada and Spain
Edited by Sue Wright
Also published as Vol. 2, No. 1 of *Current Issues in Language and Society*.
Includes bibliographical references
1. Bilingualism–Canada. 2. Multiculturalism–Canada. 3. Ethnicity–Canada.
4. Bilingualism–Spain. 5. Pluralism (Social sciences)–Spain. 6. Ethnicity–Spain.
I. Wright, Sue
P115.5.C3M66   1996
404'.2–dc20   96-11906

British Library Cataloguing in Publication Data

A CIP catalogue record for this book is available from the British Library.

ISBN 1-85359-354-0 (hbk)

Multilingual Matters Ltd

UK: Frankfurt Lodge, Clevedon Hall, Victoria Road, Clevedon, Avon BS21 7SJ.
USA: 1900 Frost Road, Suite 101, Bristol, PA 19007, USA.
Australia: P.O. Box 6025, 95 Gilles Street, Adelaide, SA 5000, Australia.

Printed and bound in Great Britain by Short Run Press.

Foreword

Julian Edge
Language Studies Unit, Aston University, Birmingham B4 7ET

The idea for this number of *Current Issues in Language and Society* began with a recollection of the opening sentence of Suzanne Romaine's book, *Bilingualism*: 'It would certainly be odd to encounter a book with the title, *Monolingualism*'. The next sentence reads:

> However, it is precisely a monolingual perspective which modern linguistic theory takes as its starting point in dealing with basic analytical problems such as the construction of grammars and the nature of competence. (Romaine, 1989: 1)

One does not need to take issue with this statement in order to assert that an equally possible second sentence might have been:

> This is because modern linguistic theory is so embedded in a monolingual perspective that the very fact that the monolingual is merely one perspective goes mostly unremarked. That which is taken for granted becomes invisible, and the consequent biases and distortions go unnoticed.

In part, these distortions arise from the equivalence of *modern* in the above quotation with *western*, and thus with what Pennycook (1994: 104) calls 'a very particular European cultural form'. He continues:

> ...an almost unquestioned premise of Western linguistics has been that monolingualism is the norm both for communities of speakers and for individuals, with bi- or multilingualism taken as an exception and often stigmatised through its connections to minority groups, the Third World, and English as a Second Language learners. (Pennycook, 1994: 136)

There is an urgent need at the heart of linguistic theorising to take account of bi- and multilingual perspectives. One approach would be to turn the techniques of linguistic inquiry back upon the monolingual premise from which they have evolved — in other words, to write the book called *Monolingualism*. One can discern various possible outlines for such a book by looking down the Contents page and substituting 'Monolingualism' for 'Bilingualism'. Thus, from a multilingual set of background assumptions, one would expect a chapter on: 'The Monolingual Brain', with sub-headings such as, 'Types of monolingualism', 'Neuro-anatomical organisation in monolinguals', and 'Monolinguals and intelligence'.

For the time being, however, it is in various contexts of applied linguistic theory that one sees more signs of movement. Kachru (1994: 796), for example, writes of the need:

> ...to re-evaluate the dominant paradigm in SLA research from a bi-/multi-

1352 0520/95/01 0001-3 $10.00/0

lingual perspective. It is especially worth examining the key notions of *native speaker*, *competence*, and *fossilisation* to show how these 'regimes of truth' (Foucault, 1972, 1980) result from a monolingual bias in SLA research.

And with reference to one of these issues, *competence*, Sridhar (1992) sketches a model of *'composite pragmatic'* competence, in which all the languages a person speaks play complementary roles in meeting their communicative needs.

It is probably not coincidental that these last two authors come to the field with an insider's awareness of multilingual beginnings, and only an outsider's knowledge of the European obsession with one-nation, one-language perceptions as the basis for awareness of self, along with the single-minded ability to pursue, in Said's (1993: 362) words: 'Identity, always identity, over and above knowing about others'.

In the field of language planning, issues of bilingualism being perceived through monolingual filters and resolved by monolingual responses have, of course, arisen before in CILS seminars. Beheydt (1994) and Nelde (1994) detail the ways in which the multilingual reality of Belgium is best seen, Brussels apart, as 'three unilingual areas ... in which the communities can independently determine their own language policies' (Beheydt, 1994: 153), and related issues are taken up in the ensuing debate. In her editorial to that issue, Wright (1994: 100) makes the telling point that:

> ...groups struggling for their rights tend to have limited objectives, usually restricted to acquiring these rights for themselves. It is an academic perspective to imagine that people fight for rights in the abstract; it is normally only their own freedom which interests them, not the parallel rights of other groups.

And we see a clear continuation of related phenomena in the current issue, where issues of monolingualism, multilingualism and identity are addressed directly in detailed studies of Canada and Spain. In the former, John Edwards tracks a steady drift towards functional monolingualism inside what may be termed the 'two solitudes' of French-speaking and English-speaking Canada:

> In a curious way, recent Canadian experience is supporting the old one-nation, one-language thesis, in contrast to the multicultural and multilingual pluralism which so many have been promoting as *the* scenario for tolerant, democratic societies.

In Spain, Hoffman highlights an emergent danger, that those regions where indigenous languages other than Castilian Spanish were long suppressed are now working to establish equally oppressive arrangements for their local language in their newly autonomous regions. At best, what may be evolving is a series of regional bilingualisms (Catalan/Castilian, Galician/Castilian, Euskera/Castilian) on a territorial principle which allows only very restricted language rights to others. Hoffman reports verbatim the most astonishing positions on bilingualism, underscored again by European obsessions with purity and identity. There seems no space here for Bhabha's (1994: 4) vision of '...the possibility of a cultural hybridity that entertains difference without an assumed or imposed hierarchy'. Hoffman's paper closes with an echo of Wright's political realism as quoted above, when she says:

> I, as a linguist, may well be much more enthusiastic about linguistic diversity and cultural pluralism than those who take political decisions and those who have to live with the consequences.

Which sentiment leaves us, perhaps, on that middle ground between description and intervention, analysis and interpretation, which is the natural area of operation of readers of this journal.

References

Beheydt, L. (1994) The linguistic situation in the new Belgium. *Current Issues in Language and Society* 1 (2), 147–63.

Bhabha, H. (1994) *The Location of Culture*. London: Routledge.

Foucault, M. (1972) *Power/Knowledge: Selected Interviews and Other Writings, 1972–1977*. (C. Gordon. 1980. Ed. and Trans.) Brighton: Harvester.

Kachru, Y. (1994) Monolingual bias in SLA research. *TESOL Quarterly* 28 (4), 795–800.

Nelde, P. (1994) Languages in contact and conflict: The Belgian experience and the European Union. *Current Issues in Language and Society* 1 (2), 165–82.

Pennycook, A. (1994) *The Cultural Politics of English as an International Language*. Harlow: Longman.

Romaine, S. (1989) *Bilingualism*. Oxford: Blackwell.

Said, E. (1993) *Culture and Imperialism*. London: Chatto and Windus. (Page references here to Vintage edition 1994).

Sridhar, S. (1992) The ecology of bilingual competence. *World Englishes* 11 (2), 141–50.

Wright, S. (1994) Editorial. *Current Issues in Language and Society* 1 (2), 99–102.

Monolingualism, Bilingualism, Multiculturalism and Identity: Lessons and Insights from Recent Canadian Experience

John Edwards
Department of Psychology, St Francis Xavier University, PO Box 5000, Antigonish,
Nova Scotia, Canada B2G 2W5

Introductory Remarks

This is a somewhat unwieldy title, I admit, but a close monitoring of events in Canada over the past few years — where both multiculturalism and bilingualism are official policies, where (however) English monolingualism remains a central feature of the daily linguistic landscape in many parts of the country, and where matters of identity are unceasingly on the agenda — reveals a fascinating and dynamic picture. Not only is this of some intrinsic interest, there are also insights here which have some generalisable value. Although the main threads of the Canadian linguistic and cultural tapestry are not unknown outside the country, the more subtle colourings, the finer strands, are not well understood; and, the devil lives in the details. My purpose, then, is twofold: to relate something of recent events in which issues of language and culture are not just riders on larger sociopolitical coat-tails — they are of the very cloth itself — and to point to those aspects of the Canadian experience which may have a broader relevance.

In this, I shall be emphasising events which have occurred between the autumns of 1992 and 1994 — i.e. from the failure of the so-called 'Charlottetown Accord' to the victory of the separatist *Parti Québécois* (PQ) in the Quebec provincial election of 12 September 1994. I can hardly do so in a vacuum, of course, but I should note at the outset that I have already written in some detail about earlier (but still recent) matters which lead into those I shall discuss here. Thus, in 'Ethnolinguistic pluralism and its discontents: A Canadian study, and some general observations' (Edwards, in press-a), I treated matters from the 1980s to the failure of the 'Meech Lake Accord' in June 1990 and its immediate aftermath; in a further, short essay appended to that (Canadian update, and rejoinder to the comments), I carried the story on to the summer of 1992; in 'The power of nationalism: The Canadian referendum of 1992' (Edwards, in press-b), I discussed events up to the failure of the Charlottetown Accord in October 1992; and, finally, in 'Language policy and planning in Canada' (Edwards, 1994a), I made a brief summary of earlier work and mentioned a few post-Charlottetown developments. These writings form the background to the present essay.

1352 0520/95/01 0005-33 $10.00/0

Constitutional Crises

In 1981–82, Canada's constitution was brought 'home' from Britain — a 'patriation' representing a final act of severance. Accompanying this was the Canadian Charter of Rights and Freedoms, one of whose parts outlined minority-language education rights meant to apply to *all* Canadians (in what was now a *constitutionally* bilingual country). Quebec saw in this a challenge to its own linguistic authority, which had steadily pushed for French dominance in the province (thus, for example, its Bill 22 (1974), which made French the official provincial language, and Bill 101 (1977), the French Language Charter). Consequently, Quebec did not sign the new constitutional accord. Still, the province was bound by the Canadian Charter, even though not a signatory, and court rulings confirmed that *that* Charter's provisions stood above those of Quebec's own (Bill 101). Thus was set in train attempts to bring Quebec into the constitutional fold, attempts which — from the outset (and before) — had to reckon with the central Québécois concerns for *survivance*, for the protection of *francophonie*.

These concerns were captured in the phrase 'a distinct society', which was the recognition Quebec demanded before rejoining, as it were, the other governments. This seemed acceptable; at Meech Lake, Quebec in 1987, all parties agreed to a 'package' which included at its core 'distinct' status for the province. But all provincial legislatures had to ratify this agreement by June 1990 — and this was not accomplished. The main ingredients of the failure were these:

(1) between 1987 and 1990 some provincial governments changed, and the existing support for the deal was not sustained;

(2) Quebec passed a law requiring all outside commercial signs to be in French only; this had an exacerbating effect upon Canadian English–French relations;

(3) in anglophone Canada, increasing concern was expressed that one province, one national group, would be designated as 'distinct' — even though the legal force of the relevant wording in the agreement was unclear. Some 'allophones', too, were affronted, and the aboriginal peoples argued that, among all Canadians, *their* society was surely the most 'distinct';

(4) nationalistic and separatist sentiment continued to grow in Quebec. If the rejection of an earlier (1980) option for 'sovereignty-association' was based, at least in part, on Québécois fears of economic stagnation, then a decade's growth of psychological and economic capital in the province had clearly and significantly reduced such apprehensions;

(5) there existed a lack of popular detailed knowledge of the Meech Lake Accord and its provisions.

After the Meech Lake failure, *new* proposals appeared and, by mid-1991, the federal government had produced a 28-point package to secure national unity. However, opposition to what were seen as special provisions for Quebec continued to harden: anglophones, allophones, disgruntled westerners, aboriginal groups and a new political organisation — the Reform Party, whose origins lay in English-speaking prairie populism — elements, at least, from all these quarters formed a sort of *ad hoc* coalition opposed to concessions (as they saw them).

Quebec upped the ante by announcing that, in the absence of satisfactory agreements, a provincial referendum on sovereignty would be held in October 1992. By August 1992, a new 'unity accord' was drafted in Charlottetown (Prince Edward Island), and it was agreed that a *national* referendum would take place on the same day (26 October) that Quebec had chosen. This accord also failed; *very* roughly, one could say that the Québécois felt it insufficiently addressed their concerns, while most of those outside the province saw it as an unacceptable *olla-podrida*.[1]

After the failure of the Charlottetown Accord, several things were clear on the Canadian political landscape. First, a general and predictable constitutional weariness gripped the country: after so much talking, so much wrangling, so many last-minute scrambles, what more could be (or should be) done? This fatigue seemed evident both within and without Quebec, although the elements comprising it naturally varied among different social and political constituencies. Second, even as many began to hope that, having twice rejected government attempts at national reconciliation, some return to 'normal' non-constitutional matters — unemployment, the economy, and so on — might be forthcoming, the realisation still nagged that Quebec–Canada arguments, with all their ramifications, would undoubtedly resurface. Third, and relatedly, the latest failure further stiffened separatist resolve in Quebec.

The *Parti Québécois* lost no time in re-predicting that an independent Quebec was the only solution to the constitutional malaise. In January 1993 Jacques Parizeau, the PQ leader, called for Quebec voters to endorse the *Bloc Québécois* (BQ) in the next federal election (the *Bloc*, led by Lucien Bouchard — who had defected from the Conservatives in May 1990 — is the *federal* party committed to Quebec independence; formed in 1990, it had eight members of parliament before the October 1993 election (see below); afterwards, it held 54 seats in Ottawa). Parizeau's call was based upon the assumption that a weak central government would provide a strong argument against federalism. An 'Italian' style of government in Ottawa would be 'extraordinarily good' for his cause, Parizeau observed (Gagnon, 1993a). Not only were these remarks seized upon in the anglophone press, they also elicited criticism in separatist circles, on two quite different grounds: first, that a fragmented Ottawa government might create difficulties for sovereigntist negotiations; second, that Parizeau's musings ought not to have been aired publicly — some noted, for example, that they highlighted the weakness and lack of political organisation of the *Bloc*.

Parizeau continued to hold centre stage when, a few days later, he outlined his timetable for independence: PQ assistance to the BQ during the next federal election (in which it was hoped that between 45 and 60 pro-sovereigntists would win seats), then a victory for the PQ in the Quebec provincial election in 1994, then a referendum on sovereignty by April 1995 and, finally, a declaration of independence on 24 June (Quebec's national holiday). Parizeau observed that, in this process, the support of Quebec anglophones and allophones was unnecessary:

> We must be perfectly conscious that Quebeckers can achieve the objective they have set for themselves, even if for the most part those who vote for it

are almost exclusively Quebeckers of old stock … Yes, we can achieve a majority … even if almost no anglophones or allophones vote for it [sovereignty]. (Séguin, 1993a)

On both issues, Parizeau's remarks elicited scorn. Writers in *La Presse*, *Le Devoir*, *Le Soleil* and other Quebec papers accused him of insensitivity and of further alienating non-francophone Quebeckers (since its beginnings in 1968, the PQ has generally failed to attract such individuals to its ranks). In fact, Parizeau's comments illuminate a longstanding issue: who are to be considered to be 'real' Quebeckers? One editorial suggested that, in talking of *les Québécois de souche*, Parizeau's 'tribal arithmetic' reduced matters to 'racial' lines. Many no doubt agreed with Quebec Premier Robert Bourassa's observation that creating two categories of citizens was not a hopeful precedent.

Bourassa and his Liberal Party were, in early 1993, reconsidering their 1988 legislation (Bill 178) which required all outside commercial signs to be in French only — their application of the famous 'notwithstanding' clause (see Edwards, in press-a) had a five-year term, a term ending on 22 December 1993. A survey conducted by the *Centre de recherches sur l'opinion publique* (CROP) now showed that 68% of Quebeckers (and, more importantly, 64% of francophone Quebeckers) were in favour of easing the restriction and of permitting bilingual signs. While the francophone majority here was reduced to 59% in Montreal and 55% in Quebec City, the more interesting breakdowns involved age and education. Thus, older and less-educated francophones were more accepting of the idea of bilingual signs than were the younger and better-educated (roughly, 78% versus 64%); it is the latter group which forms the core of the *Parti Québécois*.

Although this same conciliatory mood existed before the passage of Bill 178 — the implication being that similar volatility might also be expected five years on — most commentators agreed that, at the least, many Québécois were now concerned that the sign legislation sent an unfavourable message, that it was not what was expected of a democratic society and that, in any event, its protective force was rather slight.

Still, in preparing new language legislation, Bourassa's Liberals were re-entering a minefield. While tolerance, and the consequent willingness to see the sign law amended, were in evidence in early 1993, changes to the earlier and larger Bill 101 (the French Language Charter) were riskier. For example, many francophones were pleased with its effects on allophone children: before Bill 101, 90% of immigrant children in Montreal went to English-language schools; by 1990, two-thirds were in French ones (in the intervening years, English school enrolment dropped by 60% and about one-third of English schools — over 170 of them — closed. As it stands, only the children of those educated *in* English *in* Quebec may attend school in English). Despite this, and despite the exodus of anglophone Quebeckers, the use and status of English in the province had not declined (according to a report for the *Conseil de la langue française*, a government advisory body: see Séguin, 1993b). It is easy, then, to see that — in francophone eyes — the thrust represented by Bill 101 was still necessary.

Indeed, continuing fears of *disparition* are fuelled by immigrant arrivals, declining francophone birth rates and the use of English outside school (even where allophones are learning through French). Another study for the *Conseil*, by Marc Termote, suggested, in fact, that by the year 2000 francophone Quebeckers would comprise less than half the population of the island of Montreal (at present they constitute about 60% and 83% overall of Quebec's 6.7 million people: see Canadian Press, 1994a).

In April 1993 the *Conseil* recommended that immigrant children should continue to attend French-medium schools (the school issue remaining a 'political problem'), an unpalatable suggestion for anglophones hoping for freedom of choice and concerned about the very survival of the English system in Quebec. The *Conseil* did, however, observe that bilingual signs (with French predominant) ought to be permitted for small, independently owned businesses. Chain and department stores, however, would still be restricted to French-only external signs. Both the PQ (which, earlier in the year, had said that a sovereign Quebec would liberalise language legislation and protect anglophone minority rights) and anglophone groups were disappointed: the former, because it endorsed the *status quo*; the latter, because they felt that the relaxation did not go far enough. Claude Ryan, the minister responsible for the province's language charter, actually suggested — perhaps facetiously, for he soon recanted — that the easiest and least explosive course would be to invoke the notwithstanding clause for a further five years! In fact, by mid-April, the executive of the Liberal Party were proposing that *all* Quebec merchants be allowed to display bilingual signs (with the exceptions of billboards and other signs not on commercial premises) and urging no change to the language-of-schooling provisions.

An interesting twist occurred in late April 1993 when it was revealed that, early the previous year, the Quebec government had presented a document to the United Nations Human Rights Committee in defence of its Bill 178. This document was leaked to the media, as Premier Bourassa refused to release it (on the grounds that confidentiality had to be maintained until the UN had made a ruling). It demonstrated that, whatever their *current* position on signs, the Liberals *had* until recently held that the French collectivity required the protection afforded by Bill 178 and that, in any event, the legislation did not infringe anglophone minority rights. On 22 April 1993, the *Globe & Mail* reported obtaining a copy of the UN decision (the case, it now appeared, had been brought to the UN by 'three Quebec anglophones'; Bourassa's presentation was in response to this). The UN's response was intriguing:

> In spite of its ruling that Quebec's French-only sign violates individual rights to freedom of expression, the United Nations human-rights committee says *anglophones in the province do not constitute a minority* and therefore the law does not violate their 'minority rights'. (Séguin, 1993c: my italics)

The assumption commonly made in Canada has been, of course, that anglophones in Quebec *are* a minority in the same way as francophones elsewhere. However, the UN committee said:

> On the basis of the international definition of a minority group, the francophones of Canada, including those living in Quebec, constitute a minority within the Canadian state. And since anglophones in Quebec are part of the Canadian anglophone majority, they cannot qualify for minority-rights protection under international law. (Séguin, 1993c)

The committee made its ruling with reference to Article 27 of the International Covenant on Civil and Political Rights which, it claimed, defined minority rights within a state, not within a province of a *state*. So, the UN's recommendation that the Quebec law be changed was based upon its alleged violation of *individual* rather than *group* rights.

The Liberals were now able to claim that their position (for returning bilingual signs) was a *necessary* one. They introduced legislation (Bill 86) to amend Bill 101 in May 1993, setting off the expected debate with the PQ in the Quebec National Assembly. Camille Laurin, the 'father' of Bill 101, was blunt. He said:

> If this law passes, Quebeckers can say goodbye to a French-speaking nation. This is the beginning of a slide down a slippery slope that will lead inevitably to the destruction of the language charter. (Picard, 1993a)

And Jacques Parizeau spoke of the loss of a francophone province and a 'slide toward institutional bilingualism ... a renunciation of the effort of an entire generation to make Quebec a nation that operates in French' (Picard, 1993b). Parenthetically, I should mention here that Bill 86 was *also* to abolish the so-called 'language police' — *la commission de protection de langue française* — and to maintain the *status quo* regarding the 'francisation' of industry, whereby only companies with more than 50 employees are required to promote French as the language of the workplace). Interestingly, *Bloc Québécois* leader Lucien Bouchard declined to take part in the debate, actually favouring bilingual signs. Overall, the anti-Bill 86 rallies were rather lukewarm; most francophones endorsed change and (as noted above) the PQ was in the awkward position of opposing *now* what it had promised to do, itself, *after* independence.

Public hearings on Bill 86 were also held (from mid-May), and arguments already noted were repeatedly made. Léon Dion, a political scientist at Laval University, echoed Parizeau's remarks: 'We have entered a process that will end very soon with the complete bilingualisation of Quebec and this bill is just a step toward this end' (Seguin, 1993d). On the other hand, Guy Bertrand, a separatist and former advisor to Parizeau, supported Bill 86 on the basis that current restrictions damaged Quebec's image and interests abroad. Bill 86 was passed on 17 June 1993.

In preparation for its policy convention in late August, the PQ proposed a *new* sign-law formula: owners of small businesses (fewer than four workers) who currently have the right to English education under Bill 101 would be allowed to post bilingual signs! This idea, immediately dismissed by Claude Ryan as 'ridiculous and discriminatory', was clearly seen as bizarre by many within the PQ itself. The party proved able, at its convention, to endorse a proposal protecting anglophone rights in sovereign Quebec (see above).

On the larger Canadian stage, the autumn of 1993 saw the culmination of federal election campaigns. Of greatest interest here was the huge decline in Conservative fortunes, and the rise of the Reform Party and the *Bloc Québécois* — each of the latter capitalising on a political radicalisation within the country (and, of course, opposing one another, with Reform appealing to a populist dislike of Québécois 'agitations' and their consequences, and with the BQ building upon Quebec francophones' sense of rejection after the constitutional debacles and the feeling that a more powerful expression of Quebec self-interest was needed in Ottawa).

The election, held on 25 October 1993, saw a Liberal majority (of 177 seats, up from 80 at dissolution), the annihilation of the ruling Conservatives (down to two seats from 157 — even Kim Campbell, the new Conservative Prime Minister who had taken over from Brian Mulroney in June, lost her seat), Reform jumping from one elected member to 52, and Bouchard's BQ attaining the status of official opposition (with 54 seats; they had had eight). This official opposition in the federal parliament, it must be remembered, has as its objective the splitting of the country! 'The whisper of Quebec sovereignty,' noted one commentator, 'has become a shout that will echo through Canada's Parliament and haunt the staunchly federalist Liberal government' (Picard, 1993c). Lucien Bouchard observed that 'the true face' of Canada had finally emerged. He also noted that the BQ's *raison d'être* would not disrupt parliament, nor would his *Bloc* be anything other than a good opposition — for as long as the country might last in its current state (Séguin, 1993e). A piece in *The Economist* saw in the election of the BQ a clear portent of separation. Yet, while recognising that costs existed (and that the rest of the world — 'a gleeful France excepted' — would not wish for Quebec independence), the article suggested that 'separation would do Canada no great harm ... [it] would be sad, but bearable' (*Globe & Mail*, 1993).

The next stage, then, was the provincial election in Quebec where, with the assistance of the now-powerful BQ, Parizeau's PQ were already being touted to oust Bourassa's Liberals. As well, a new party of 'moderate nationalism' — committed to work for partnership between Canada and an independent Quebec — came into being in December 1993. This *Parti Action Québec* was interested in some European-style supranational parliamentary arrangements linking Canada and Quebec, arrangements which (it was believed) Quebeckers would insist upon before voting for independence. Whether this revival of the idea of sovereignty-association would result in votes taken from the Liberals or the PQ was, of course, an immediate consideration.

While the new PAQ was attempting to rejuvenate the political accommodation first suggested by René Lévesque (the PQ's original leader), Lucien Bouchard was making clear, on a visit of 'reassurance' to Washington, that the BQ was a *separatist* party. Among PQ members, Parizeau had never shied away from the term, although others had retained some philosophical links with 'sovereignty-association', with its connotations of *both* political independence *and* economic association. Other words, too, have been seen to possess various nuances. For example, *indépendantiste* was understood in Quebec to have a more neutral sense than *séparatiste* (federal politicians having been fond of the insulting term, *méchant séparatiste*). Words, as always, are important in Quebec political life — as, of course, they are elsewhere — and the use of (say) *indépendantiste* instead of *séparatiste* might have significant effects in debates, polls and referenda.

A poll taken in early March 1994 by *Groupe Léger et Léger* reinforces this observation: asked if Quebec sovereignty and separation meant the same thing, or were 'two different issues', 58% of Quebeckers indicated the latter, 37% the former, and only 5% said they didn't know. This last, small percentage is interesting given a terminological inexactitude often exacerbated for particular political ends. For example, some have argued that sovereignty means independence, while others note that Quebec (as other provinces) is sovereign *now*, within its constitutional jurisdiction. Jean-Marc Léger suggested that the results of the March poll meant that most wanted to retain ties with the rest of Canada:

> What is important is that in people's minds the concept of sovereignty is a positive one; it implies maintaining a relationship with the rest of Canada. The poll also suggests that the word 'separation' is a very negative word in Quebec … It suggests breaking all links with the rest of Canada. (Mackie, 1994a)

Of course, the question of what is important (or understood) in people's minds at polling time is a very large one. A final point here: it is noteworthy that the percentages cited above were remarkably consistent across age, sex and linguistic groups, among pro- and anti-sovereigntists, and among Liberals and members of the PQ (total sample was 1003 respondents).

Other polls in the spring of 1994 predicted a PQ sweep in the upcoming provincial election and the party, encouraged by these, distributed across Canada a magazine containing its post-victory agenda. Among its points were a commitment to native representation in the National Assembly and native involvement in the preparation of a new Quebec constitution, a determination to assist immigrants to integrate and succeed in Quebec, in French, and five assurances to anglophones; the PQ would:

(1) guarantee in the constitution the right to speak English in the courts and in the National Assembly;
(2) guarantee the right to an anglophone school system controlled by anglophones;
(3) maintain and protect the social and health services of the anglophone community;
(4) institute a program of access to jobs in the public service for anglophones;
(5) maintain public radio and television networks in the English language. (Mackie, 1994b).

At this time, too, a 1992 survey was publicised, a survey of some 4000 anglophone students in Montreal. It showed 79% accepting the necessity of bilingualism and 87% agreeing that the position of English was deteriorating (but see, above, the reports for the *Conseil de la langue française*). In strictly demographic terms, English *is* on the wane. Between 1976 (when the PQ first came to power) and 1991, those with English as mother tongue declined from about 800,000 to 670,000 in the province. In the Montreal region the anglophone community now represents about 15% of the population (almost an identical presence to that of the allophones). Most predictions are for further decline (and, for example, in the 1992 survey just cited, only 21% expected to remain in Quebec: see Mackie, 1994c).

A CROP poll in late March indicated that 38% of Quebeckers would vote for the PQ, 33% for the Liberals (among francophones, these percentages became 57% and 33% respectively). Since Liberal votes are heavily concentrated in a few Montreal constituencies, the suggestions were of a strong PQ victory. Interestingly, however, support for party *leaders* was reversed: 44% in favour of Daniel Johnson (who took over from Bourassa in January 1994) and 29% for Jacques Parizeau (who had consistently run behind his party in public opinion: see Mackie, 1994b).

Such polls began to concentrate minds, both within and without Quebec. Bouchard, on a trip to France and Belgium (which infuriated many in Canada, but which had virtually no impact in Europe) claimed that Ottawa, while it would be forced to respect the outcome of a referendum, would try to block international recognition of an independent Quebec (see Gagnon, 1994b, for a discussion of the symbolic, historic and essentially 'special' ties between Quebec and France, ties which were strikingly brought to the attention of anglophone Canada by Charles de Gaulle's famous peroration of 1967, *'vive le Québec libre'* — and now, Gagnon suggests, by Lucien Bouchard 27 years later).

The French were cautious: René Monory, president of the Senate, gave Bouchard (who was once Canadian ambassador to France) a warm welcome, noting that 'if the people of Quebec and all of Canada recognize Quebec's independence, there is no reason why we wouldn't recognize Quebec' (Koring, 1994b). Similarly, the former French Premier, Michel Rocard, gave a 'heavily hedged' endorsement according to Koring (1994c): 'if [he said] a separatist party wins the next election in Quebec, and if a referendum endorses independence, then [he hoped] France will rally international support for recognition of Quebec.' This hardly seems the 'gleeful' response to possible independence which *The Economist* suggested was typical of France (see above), or any great reincarnation of (de) Gaullist sentiment. Bouchard did report receiving, privately, many assurances of support for Quebec independence, however.

From western Canada in particular, politicians warned that Quebec secession would be neither painless nor amicable. In some eyes, Bouchard's position in Ottawa — of leading an official opposition committed to the secession of part of the state — was that of a traitor (see Alberta Premier Ralph Klein's discussion with radio host Rafe Mair, as reported by Cernetig, 1994). Nor, it was pointed out, could Quebec necessarily expect to leave with all the territory currently held as a province (see also below). The tenor of many comments is captured in the following:

> Like it or not, the battle of Quebec has already begun. There is no sense now in sparing the sensibilities of Quebeckers, or anyone else. Politicians outside Quebec — including the Prime Minister — have a right and a responsibility to say frankly what separation would bring. They have a right and responsibility to expose the smooth but reckless games of the separatist leaders. They have a right and a responsibility to reaffirm, again and again, the superiority of federation (*Globe & Mail*, 1994a).

Whatever one may think of the last two sentences, this leader's tone reflected that of a country in which (unlike at the time of the 1980 referendum) conciliation seemed unlikely. Still, in late May, Prime Minister Jean Chrétien announced himself reluctant to join in the debate. While some claimed that this stance was a dereliction of federal duty, it seemed to others that, by representing (or, at least, appearing to represent) a relatively unchanged federalist 'option', Chrétien on the offensive could actually strengthen the separatist hand. Reform Party leader Preston Manning's solution was that the forces for unity ought not to allow the question to devolve to one of separation or the *status quo*. He claimed that a fully reworked federal 'vision' was required; this would have the advantage of providing Quebeckers with an acceptable alternative to separatism while, at the same time, addressing other issues of importance in other provinces and sectors of society. And, within Quebec, Daniel Johnson announced his election strategy in June. After having insisted that the economy was the real issue for Quebeckers, he now stated that sovereignty would be the main focus. This changed tack was seen as risky, for the reason noted above (with regard to Chrétien's stance: see comments assembled by Picard, 1994b).

While anglophones and federalists agonised over what action, if any, was required in the run-up to the Quebec election, *La Presse* columnist Lysiane Gagnon advised calm; her comments here reflect both a careful analysis of contemporary events and an understanding of how Quebeckers have, in the past, typically hedged their political bets:

> The fact is that Quebec voters don't mind having a sovereigntist govern-ment in Quebec City, but they are not about to vote for sovereignty. Illogical? Perhaps, but who ever said politics is pure reason ... the proportion of voters who would vote for sovereignty still hovers around 40 per cent. And the proportion of 'Yes' voters shrinks by several points when it's made clear that sovereignty means independence and separation. Moreover, poll after poll shows that despite what the political class says, Quebec voters have already decided that the coming election will *not* be about sovereignty. This is a strong, massive resolution, shared by even a majority of those who intend to vote for the PQ. Over the years, there have been short periods when the separatist barometer rose sharply — after the failure of the Meech Lake accord, for instance. But this happened only when there was no 'danger' ahead, no real vote to be taken, no radical leader in power. (Gagnon, 1994c)

In mid-June, the spring sitting of Quebec's National Assembly ended, and activity predicated on a summer election campaign began. A *Léger et Léger* poll found, in mid-July, that support for the PQ stood at 51%, compared with 42% for the Liberals; however, support for *sovereignty* declined (and *sovereignty* has proved a term more likely to attract votes than either *separation* or *independence* would do: Mackie, 1994e). Other questions revealed continuing confusion about the meaning of 'a sovereign Quebec'. For example, while 61% agreed that such a state would no longer pay taxes to Ottawa, 41% thought it would still use Canadian passports and, in short, continue to be part of Canada (Mackie, 1994d).

On 24 July 1994, Premier Johnson finally called the election — for 12 September. While there remained the vexing question of just what Quebeckers wanted, the choice presented to them of either a federalist party or a separatist one was remarkably clear. Parizeau, for his part, pointed out that if victorious he would govern the province as if it were already independent and that, indeed, the election battle would be a rehearsal of the arguments for independence; for the referendum he still promised to hold within ten months of assuming the premiership. This was generally well-understood, particularly in western Canada where feelings of 'let's get it all over with' were not unrelated to desires for a broader, reworked federalism (and, indeed, to a minor revival of separatist sentiment in the west itself). In Quebec, though, there was a curious lassitude, causing observers to speculate that, once again, the voters were more interested in a change of government than in independence, that they would elect separatists but, at the final hurdle, would vote 'no' in the referendum, that (in short) they would again edge towards independence and then balk (see Gagnon, above).

Given, however, that the party differences were so clearly defined this time, and given that a PQ government would be in a powerful position to push for independence in the run-up to the referendum, it was thought that the momentum might prove sufficient — this time — to carry the electorate over that last fence. That is why the Liberals unceasingly hammered at the sovereignty issue during the campaign; as Mackie (1994f) put it, 'Mr Johnson's task is to persuade voters who are supporting the *Parti Québécois* because they want a change in government and not because they want independence that it would be too dangerous to elect the party.' The PQ, on the other hand, aware of the questions in voters' minds, stressed that good government and economic improvement should be the *immediate* priority. Of course, sovereignty inevitably took centre stage anyway — even Parizeau himself acknowledged this when (for example), speaking to fishermen in the Gaspé, he pointed out that good government would be best achieved through independence.

In early August, internal difficulties in the separatist camp emerged. Generally, Parizeau favoured the opening of 'discussions' with Canada, and the passage of a 'pro-sovereignty declaration' in the National Assembly, immediately after the election. The BQ, on the other hand, endorsed a more measured approach; in particular, Bouchard (much more popular, personally, than Parizeau, by the way; the latter acknowledged that he was a 'technician' of independence and not the 'conscience' of nationalism embodied in the PQ's founder, René Lévesque) rejected the idea that the National Assembly itself could assume a pro-independence stance before the referendum.

During the election campaign, opinion polling was virtually continuous. One survey, which seemed to provide good news for the Liberals, was conducted by CROP between 28 July and 2 August; it showed them at 46% (to the PQ's 48%). Picard's analysis, however, puts these apparently neck-and-neck figures into perspective:

> In reality, the two-point difference in the poll with a 3% margin of error would translate into about 80 seats for the Péquistes in the 125-seat National Assembly — a very comfortable majority. The overall popularity of the party is largely irrelevant because of the linguistic breakdown of the vote and the different voting patterns among French and non-French speakers. Province-wide, Liberals attract an astonishing 80% of the non-francophone vote, but only 32% of the francophone vote. The PQ, on the other hand, grabbed a slender 7% of allophones and 49% of francophones. And the number that really counts is not found in the poll: the 1991 Census tells us that 82% of Quebeckers are francophones. (Picard, 1994c)

Further analysis suggested that — in anglophone eyes, anyway — the Quebec electorate were poised to vote 'illogically' for a party with the least popular leader (Parizeau), which failed to stress the issues commonly deemed the most important (i.e. economic ones) and which was openly committed to independence (which a majority do not endorse). Why? Weariness with nine years of Liberal rule, the desire for change and the hope that, after all, the PQ might provide new impetus seemed to be the answer. Some PQ analysts themselves accepted this and acknowledged, therefore, that their main task after electoral victory would be to swing the population firmly over to independence. Stéphane Dion, however, a political scientist at the University of Montreal, argued that as the deadline (the referendum) approached, support for separatism would decline. Quebeckers were currently able, as in the past, to think of sovereignty as a form of autonomy *within* Canada; but, the realisation that this option is no longer on offer from the PQ would increasingly weaken resolve to make the ultimate act of severance. Indeed, Dion claimed that harping on sovereignty might be costly for the PQ in the provincial election itself. While, in the elections of 1976 and 1981, René Lévesque had made it clear that he would work for Quebec, sovereign or not, people were now asking themselves (said Dion) if Parizeau would be very interested in managing a province (see Winsor, 1994a).

Just before the election, speculation arose over the PQ's hint that, were they to lose the referendum on sovereignty, they would hold a second one. The spectre of endless attempts and endless tension, until the 'right' verdict arrived, was not a pleasant one. Lysiane Gagnon, however, noted that, privately, Quebec separatists acknowledged that, given all their current advantages, the referendum was, in effect, the *dernière chance*:

> The Parti Québécois is coming to power as the economy recovers; after the double failure of the Meech and Charlottetown accords, there can be no hope for significant constitutional reform; the Quebec government will be led by a man who is a much tougher and more Machiavellian strategist than Mr Lévesque; with the help of Lucien Bouchard's Bloc Québécois, the separatist movement will send a formidable team up against a weak federalist camp — Prime Minister Jean Chrétien will never have the impact that Pierre Trudeau had in 1980, and Premier Daniel Johnson's credibility will be badly damaged after what promises to be a resounding defeat. If, in such a favourable context and with all these assets in hand, the PQ loses the 1995 referendum, it would be more than a crushing defeat: it would be the last chapter in the present generation's book. (Gagnon, 1994d)

On Monday 12 September, the PQ won the Quebec election, taking 77 seats to the Liberal's 47 — although their share of the popular vote was only 0.6% greater (44.8% versus 44.2%). Another 6.5% of the vote (and one seat in the National Assembly) went to the *Parti Action Démocratique du Québec* (the former *Parti Action Québec*). Seeing the defeat to be less overwhelming than expected, both the provincial and federal Liberals immediately warned the PQ not to delay or avoid the promised referendum.

The results put the PQ back into power with roughly the same standing they had when first elected in 1976, as Table 1 indicates. Figures provided immediately

Table 1 Recent Quebec election results

Election	Seats won: PQ	Popular vote :Liberal
November 1976	71 (41%)	26 (34%)
April 1981	80 (49%)	42 (46%)
December 1985	23 (39%)	99 (56%)
September 1989	29 (40%)	92 (50%)

Note: This table appeared in slightly altered form in the *Globe & Mail* where, however, the standings of Liberals and PQ in the 1981 election were reversed by mistake: see also Dion (1992)

Table 2 Changing support for concepts of sovereignty

Time period	Percentage level of support for:				
	Sep.	*Ind.*	*Sov.*	*Sov.-Ass.*	*Sov-Ass. (Neg)*
1960–1964	8	-	-	-	-
1965–1969	10	-	-	-	-
1970–1974	13	27	-	32	-
1975–1979	19	20	-	31	49
1980–1985	-	20	18	39	40
1986–1989	37	32	41	46	-
1990	44	50	55	58	68
1991	42	46	53	60	-
1992	33	40	45	58	-
1993	33	39	49	58	-

Note: Sep. = Separatism; Ind = Independence; Sov. = Sovereignty; Sov.-Ass. = Sovereignty-Association; Sov.Ass. (Neg.) = Mandate to negotiate Sovereignty-Association

after the election by Winsor (1994b) — drawing upon the work of Cloutier, Gay & Latouche (1992) and Lisée (1994) — allow us to chart the changing levels of support for the five different sovereignty 'concepts'. These figures (see Table 2) are based upon analyses of 165 polls taken since 1960.

Winsor suggested that the failure of the Meech Lake agreement (in June 1990) was the single biggest boost to separatist sentiment since (but exceeding) the first election of the PQ in 1976. However, this type of support dropped from 1990–91 peaks before the present election call, and continued to decline over the 50-day campaign. Thus, the most recent poll showed 59% opposed to sovereignty —

virtually identical to the 60% opposing it in the 1980 referendum (on the 'softer' proposition of the *negotiation* of sovereignty-association). Cloutier *et al.* (1992) argued, from a pro-independence position, that the post-Meech surge would prove the springboard to sovereignty. Stéphane Dion (1992), looking at the same figures, analysed the situation along three lines: Quebec's sense of the fragility of French in North America (and the centrality of language in Quebec nationalism), the confidence among the Québécois as *maîtres chez eux*, and the catalyst which the Meech Lake failure provided for perceived rejection by English Canada. It is clear, I think, that all three factors subtly intertwine and contribute to the volatility of separatist sentiment in Quebec.

A final post-election observation: between mid-January 1994 and the election there were more than 25 surveys of Quebec political opinion conducted by professional polling bodies; half of these were carried out during the official election period itself. While some variation was, naturally enough, detected, the earliest polls tallied remarkably well with the most recent; for example, a *Léger et Léger* survey in mid-January showed the PQ with 88 seats (and 46.6% of the popular vote), the Liberals with 37 (40.9%). A poll by the same firm, taken between 30 August and 1 September, suggested exactly the same number of seats for each party (although the popular vote percentages had changed to 49% and 42.6%). Given the usual margin of error (of about plus/minus three percentage points), it can be seen that the earlier survey was more accurate than the later (although a CROP poll of 1–3 September did predict that the PQ would receive 46% of the vote, the Liberals 43%, which is more accurate than either). The actual final result showed, of course, the two parties virtually equal in votes received; it is because of the high concentration of Liberal votes in the anglophone and allophone areas around Montreal (about 30 constituencies) that this equality translated into the PQ's 30-seat majority in the National Assembly.

Political Overviews

Fuller analyses of the Quebec–Canada issue have, of course, begun to appear. For example, Mordecai Richler, a prominent Canadian novelist, had written on the subject as early as 1983, when he provided a personal view of the rise of the PQ under René Lévesque and the failed referendum on sovereignty-association of May 1980. Then, in a long article in the *New Yorker* (1991), Richler carried the story forward to the aftermath of Meech Lake (a story expanded in his book of 1992). His own position, generally, is one of opposition to Quebec nationalism. Most recently (again, in the *New Yorker*, 1994), Richler painted a picture of social and economic turmoil and an accelerated exodus of anglophones from Quebec, should separation occur.

Philip Resnick, whose earlier book (1991) advocated radical change, and suggested that greater social democracy could emerge in a Canada without Quebec, returned to the issue in 1994. Arguing that separation may well occur, Resnick supported a renewed *English*-Canadian nationalism, a renewed sense of anglophone identity. In 1991, Bercuson & Cooper wrote that Canada and Quebec ought to go their separate ways. While Resnick had argued that a Canada free of Quebec — with its free-enterprise support of North American trade — could better resist strident Americanisation, Bercuson & Cooper's thesis was that such a Canada would be free — once the politically irritating and financially draining Quebec had left — to move more firmly to the *right*. As Simpson (1991) pointed out in a review, both analyses cannot be correct, even though both agree that separation ought to occur:

> *Deconfederation* [the title of Bercuson & Cooper's book] is grotesquely one-dimensional political science, unimpressive political theory, slanted history. It's based on low levels of academic analysis and high levels of emotional content. But in a perverse way, *Deconfederation* is worth a read. It shows how the right and left in English-speaking Canada share the same disillusionment with Quebec. It faithfully reflects a certain accusatory view towards Quebec prevalent in English-speaking Canada. (Simpson, 1991)

Bercuson returned to his thesis directly after the 12 September election, noting that, now, secession was inevitable:

> English-speaking Canadians must either give up the quest to create a liberal democracy of multi-ethnic origin, or they must wave goodbye to Quebec. Since they will not do the first (the October 1992 referendum is proof enough of that), they must sooner or later do the second. (Bercuson, 1994)

According to Bercuson, secession should in fact be a part of a major *Canadian* reorganisation (which, incidentally, ought never to countenance a Quebec which *unilaterally* declared independence). In the short term, Bercuson claimed, separatism will exact a high price: recession, inflation and lowered living standards. But, overall, an unfettered Canada will thrive (see Cook, 1994, for a brief rejoinder to this thesis).

In a book published by the conservative Fraser Institute, Gordon Gibson (1994) — a Liberal westerner — urged careful consideration of the possibility of Quebec separation. While hoping that further negotiation might yet avert this, Gibson sketched a picture of a post-separation Canada plagued by regional fissiparous tendencies, and a dramatically altered federal government in Ottawa. An American commentator, Lansing Lamont, has also produced a book (1994) dealing with the consequences of rupture. Almost all imaginable woes are detailed here, including a fractured rest-of-Canada seeking a new and closer association with the United States, American military intervention and increased pressure on *francophonie* in the North American anglophone sea.

More rounded commentaries have been provided by Taylor (1993) and Simpson (1993). The former, a well-known philosopher, presents a collection of previously-published essays which is notable for its adherence to the Augustinian injunction, *audi partem alteram*. A federalist himself, Taylor concludes by suggesting a new federalist arrangement, a 'broader Canadian frame' within which could exist two major societies, internally diverse themselves. Simpson's (1993) hope is also for a better thought-out but still united Canada, and his book comprises the 'ideas and life stories' of eight prominent Canadians — among them, Preston Manning (leader of the Reform Party), Clyde Wells (the Newfoundland premier whose Meech Lake role was so important), Georges Erasmus (of the Assembly of First Nations) and Lucien Bouchard — all of whom hold strong views on current issues.

There is, of course, a wider literature in the journals which details the background to the Quebec–Canada issue (and, to some extent, the thrust of current events). Also, full-length treatments of *aspects* of these events have begun to appear (see, particularly, the very useful collection prompted by the failure of the Charlottetown Accord: McRoberts & Monahan, 1993). However, for present purposes — to provide an overview of the broader picture — the works cited in this short section give an idea of how this wider perspective has been approached.

Economics and Sovereignty

One of the planks in the federalist platform has, consistently, been the costs of Quebec separation. Conversely, the PQ has argued that independence would make good economic sense. And all agree that the current state of uncertainty is economically damaging.

A dire report was issued in June 1994 by DRI Canada; it forecast a Canadian dollar worth 0.67 American (the current rate is about 0.72), a prime lending rate of 10% (currently 6.5%) and the loss of 20,000 jobs if the PQ were to win the election and then hold a referendum in 1995. The DRI study was discussed by Little (1994), who also referred to allegations that PQ members had told economists to downplay possible costs (and, in some cases, had threatened to take business away from 'negative' bond underwriters and brokers; Jacques Parizeau himself denounced as 'meddling' statements by the Bank of Montreal that sovereignty would undoubtedly mean a lower dollar, higher interest rates and loss of international investment). Raymond Théoret, a Quebec economist, predicted 'a decade of economic pain'. And, in a 1992 report, the chairman of the Royal Bank had argued that costs would be 'huge and long term ... paid by people in every province for generations to come' (Davidson, 1994).

One concrete example of uncertainty was the Japanese 'unloading' of some $3.5 billion in Canadian-dollar securities, reported in mid-June 1994. This was directly linked to fears for the future (it is true that most of the sell-off was then bought by *American* investors, but they demanded a high premium on those bonds; furthermore, American firms were advising their clients to delay buying Canadian bonds, at least until after the election).

An independent Quebec would want to join the North American Free Trade Agreement (NAFTA, which currently links Canada, Mexico and the United States), and Parizeau reported that on a trip to Washington in 1993 he was told that the Americans would not block Quebec entry. However, any such entry would clearly require renegotiation. Since NAFTA came into effect in January 1989, Quebec exports to the United States have in fact outpaced those from the rest of the country, a fact demonstrating (in separatist eyes) that Quebec would be a viable independent state. On the other hand, the Wall Street Journal observed that:

> Quebec had the worst GDP growth of Canada's regions in 1992 and 1993: under 1% GDP growth over that two-year period, versus 3% for all of Canada. Including Quebec's share of the national government's $300 billion in financial-market debt, Quebec is now the industrialized world's biggest

state debtor relative to savings, and the biggest combined net importer of goods, services and investment relative to the size of the economy. Indeed, Quebec accounts for half of Canada's current-account deficit, although it has only a quarter of Canada's population (Blohm, 1994).

As can be imagined, figures and statistics were bandied about by all sides. For example, Premier Daniel Johnson claimed that separation would cost $8 billion because of withdrawal from federal–provincial cost-sharing programmes. Parizeau asserted that sovereignty would be less expensive than the $281 million spent to date on constitutional meetings, commissions and conferences! The same Royal Bank which had issued the frightening 1992 report predicted, in August 1994, that Quebec economic growth would *exceed* Canada's in 1995 — even with a PQ election victory. The Fraser Institute in Vancouver warned of debt-induced catastrophe, while the American brokerage firm, Salomon Brothers, claimed that *uncertainty* was the culprit, and that a resolution for *either* unity or separation would lead to stability in the bond markets (however, it should be noted that Salomon Brothers, so often approvingly cited by Parizeau, were scrambling to regain their lost leadership of the underwriting business; they sell Quebec bonds, and would like to sell more). And, in one market at least — that of 'short-term paper' — foreign investors were profiting from the Canadian economic uncertainty and the consequent gap between American and Canadian interest rates. Running through all this was the central question: how much of the overall Canadian debt would a departing Quebec assume? (If population proportion were to be the key here, then Quebec would leave with a quarter of the burden, a share amounting to $150 billion.)

By election day, when many became convinced that the PQ would indeed win but that their 1995 referendum would fail, a bond rally was predicted. The day *after* the election, the dollar climbed by more than a cent, a buying rally pushed up the value of stocks and bonds, and interest rates declined.

Whatever the state of the market, and whatever the costs associated with separation, few would deny the ever-increasing control francophones have asserted over their own economic destiny. A study by François Vaillancourt and Michel Leblanc revealed that 65% of the provincial economy was in the hands of francophones by 1991 (as opposed to 47% thirty years earlier); now, 26% and 9% of control is exercised by English Canadians and foreign firms, respectively (in 1961, their combined control amounted to 53%: see McKenna, 1993). This greater economic power, and a greater possibility, at least, of the viability of an independent Quebec than had been evident at the time of the earlier referendum (in 1980), have fuelled separatist hopes. Naturally, no one can say what the future holds; not only are economic matters difficult to predict in general, but the circumstances of a Quebec secession — chiefly, the debt load it would assume — are, of course, yet to be negotiated.

Aboriginal Issues and Quebec Territoriality[2]

Aboriginal issues continued to be an important part of the Quebec–Canada debate during 1994. Most aspects centred upon the 'distinct' society aimed at by Quebec nationalists but to be denied, apparently, to natives. The prospect of being taken into a separate country by francophone Québécois was an unattractive one in many aboriginal eyes; it also prompted questions about the federal stance *vis-à-vis* a Quebec minority unwilling to secede (on PQ terms, at least). A good deal of broad public sympathy existed for aboriginal groups and claims during the 1992 Charlottetown Accord debate, and recent polls suggest that this has not abated; one found that 75% of Canadians were in support of aboriginal self-government. Many, then, asked why Quebec native groups should not have the right to choose their own future. If Quebec could separate, why should it make its native population unwilling victims of the break?

Within Quebec, discussions of aboriginal autonomy were 'criminalised' by a press and public anti-native to the point of racism (according to Bruno Bisson of *La Presse*); this sentiment was, perhaps, the inevitable outcome of a clash between two nationalist movements, and was certainly exacerbated during the violent Oka crisis of 1990, in which an armed stand-off had existed for much of the summer between Montreal-area Mohawks and Quebec authorities (Picard, 1994a; however Gagnon, 1994a, cites a report showing that Quebec natives have fared better than those elsewhere — in terms of social conditions, education and language retention).

In May 1994, federal Indian Affairs Minister Ron Irwin declared bluntly that aboriginal Quebeckers have the right to remain in Canada in the event of separation. Bouchard, on his European trip, quickly replied that Quebec's territorial integrity was 'sacred', that no sections of the province could be 'clawed back' and that any attempt to change provincial boundaries would 'turn even francophone federalists into arch-nationalists' (Koring, 1994a). Now, while there is no necessary link between some intra-provincial carve-up and continued federal rights for Quebec aboriginal groups — there might, after all, be federally administered enclaves within a separate Quebec (although, admittedly, this could prove very unwieldy) — Bouchard went on to note that 'native people do not have the right to self-determination … it [Quebec] does not belong to them. We have been very clear on that, on legal grounds.' In the same report, however, Prime Minister Chrétien observed that, if Quebec were to decide to separate, all views of territorial integrity would be subject to negotiation (Delacourt, 1994).

PQ claims on territoriality were bolstered by opinions solicited from experts in international law. However, an interesting analysis was provided by Patrick Monahan, an Osgoode Hall lawyer:

> [The experts cited by the PQ] were of the view that, *on the assumption that Quebec has already attained sovereignty*, aboriginal peoples living in Quebec would have no right under international law to secede from an independent Quebec … The reason was simply that only 'colonial peoples' — people living in a defined territory under the control of a foreign power — have a right to secede under international law. Aboriginal peoples living in Quebec do not meet that definition; but, said the experts, explicitly, *neither do Quebeckers themselves*. Thus, while international law would not recognise a right of aboriginal peoples to secede from Quebec, neither would it recognise any right of Quebec secession from Canada. If Mr Parizeau wants to deny aboriginal peoples a right to secede based on international law

principles, he must also concede that Quebec itself has no such right. (Monahan, 1994; original italics)

On the question of territorial integrity, Monahan noted that international recognition often depends upon the political effectiveness of secession — 'whether the political authorities in the seceding state can exert effective political control over the territory and population to which they lay claim.' He went on:

> This analysis is totally at odds with Mr Parizeau's assertion that international law somehow supports Quebec's claim to its current borders after sovereignty. In fact, it says the opposite. If natives in northern Quebec refuse to recognize the authority of the new Quebec state, Quebec will be unable to lay claim to that territory unless it can, through the exercise of force if required, demonstrate that it has effective control over it. (Monahan, 1994)

It can be added here that Quebec territorial discussions do not hinge upon native land claims alone; a larger issue has to do with historical change. The boundaries of the province have altered half a dozen times since the middle of the eighteenth century — from *la nouvelle France*, to Lower Canada, to the loss of the Labrador coast (to Newfoundland), to the acquisition of Rupert's Land and Ungava. Might an independent Quebec retain the monarchy to maintain its trusteeship of its northern regions? Would native constitutional and land claims have some legal status? And what of the anglophone pockets in the western part of the province, in the *Cantons de l'Est* and on the island of Montreal — a population of three-quarters of a million, ten times larger than that of the 11 aboriginal nations recognised in Quebec — what arrangements could or should be made for them?

Still, for the moment at least, native claims represent the most likely point of contention. While BQ leader Bouchard was dismissing aboriginal demands, it was revealed that, in 1992, an expert on international law *within* the PQ — Daniel Turp — had written:

> The native nations are in a position similar to that of the Québécois when it comes to invoking international law in support of the claim that they have the right to self-determination ... In view of the 'nation' status of the native communities, unequivocally affirmed by their representatives and explicitly recognised by Quebec in the resolution of its National Assembly ... they may justifiably invoke for their own benefit the same international instruments as the Québécois ... the aboriginal nations are free to choose from several options, including complete sovereignty, remaining in Quebec, or remaining in Canada if Quebec separates. (York, 1994)

In May 1994, Turp claimed to agree with Bouchard, arguing that earlier he had made a 'liberal and generous' interpretation of aboriginal rights (nonetheless, Bouchard now admitted that the aboriginal question was 'very delicate ... very sophisticated'). Bouchard's admission is quite obviously true. The Royal Commission on Aboriginal Peoples (established in August 1991) had, by January 1994, heard 2200 submissions in over one hundred communities, had spent about $25 million and had amassed some 60,000 pages of official transcript. Furthermore, talks on native self-government among Ottawa, the provinces and five native groups (the Inuit Tapirisat, the Métis National Council, the Congress of Aboriginal Peoples, the Native Women's Association and the Assembly of First Nations) fell into disarray when the last-named organisation (representing 400,000 status Indians) withdrew from a two-day meeting in mid-May 1994. The issue was the AFN's call for legal and constitutional recognition at the federal level, not merely the 'administrative agreements' proposed by Ottawa and the provinces. In August 1994, the Cree of northern Quebec announced that *they* would hold a referendum if the PQ won the election on 12 September; native voters would be asked to opt for remaining with Canada, going with an independent Quebec, or becoming sovereign themselves (i.e. the same choices outlined by Turp in 1992).

If Turp's 1992 comments about native rights had stirred the pot when made public, then another 1992 statement — by Richard Le Hir, a PQ candidate — also created an outburst when *it* was released (in August 1994). Speaking of the Cree in Quebec, Le Hir said that native cultures have nothing to teach modern society:

> I would have something to learn from them if it could be shown that their culture demonstrated its superiority in one form or another ... [but] when you look at what heritage has been left by native civilizations — if you could call them civilizations — there is very little. (Canadian Press, 1994b)

Bilingualism

Canada has been officially bilingual since the Official Languages Act of 1969 (revised and updated in 1988), the main thrust of which was institutional bilingualism and the provision of official services in both French and English. No individual was required to become bilingual — apart from civil servants — although personal bilingualism was seen as desirable and to be encouraged. Provisions were made for official minority-language children to be educated in their mother tongue wherever numbers warranted (as might be expected, implementing this policy has often proved to be contentious). Yet, in his report on the quindecennial of the Act, the Commissioner of Official Languages noted the polarisation of various linguistic groups and the 'peripheral' nature of bilingualism for 'the great majority of Canadians' (Fortier, 1985: 3; see also Héroux, 1990). As a policy, federal bilingualism — bearing in mind its 'peripheral' status — has received passive acceptance, although resentment against its manifestations has always been apparent in some quarters, particularly in regions further removed from Quebec. Quebec itself, of course, has steadily supported French dominance, and recent crises have made bilingualism a representation of the Quebec–Canada conflict.

It is useful to recall here that the Commission on Bilingualism and Biculturalism, whose deliberations during the 1960s gave rise to the Official Languages Act, had closely examined the so-called 'personality' and 'territorial' principles (see Nelde, Labrie & Williams, 1992). In the first, linguistic rights are seen to inhere in individuals, wherever they may live within a state (as in South Africa). According to the territorial principle (as in Belgium), however, rights vary regionally, and the linguistic arrangement is commonly a type of 'twinned'

Table 3 Percentage of Canadians of French mother tongue who have shifted to English as a home language, by province or territory, 1977 and 1981

Region	1971	1981
British Columbia	73.0	71.8
Alberta	53.7	57.0
Saskatchewan	51.9	63.4
Manitoba	36.9	44.0
Ontario	29.9	33.9
Quebec	1.5	2.0
New Brunswick	8.7	9.7
Nova Scotia	34.1	37.1
Prince Edward Island	43.2	42.1
Newfoundland	43.4	57.2
Yukon	74.4	70.2
Northwest Territories	51.3	54.5
Canada as a whole	6.0	6.7
Canada minus Quebec	29.6	32.8

Source: Fortier (1985). Based upon 1971 and 1981 Statistics Canada census figures.

unilingualism. Despite the fact that the Commissioners — and, subsequently, the government — opted for the personality principle in Canada, recent developments and demographic trends have increasingly brought about a *de facto* territorialism. Thus, francophones outside Quebec and anglophones within it have undergone language shift (or have moved). Dreams of a bilingual country have faded, and we have seen the continuing emergence of twinned unilingualisms in Quebec and the rest of the country, with a 'bilingual belt' in parts of Ontario and New Brunswick. In his cogent review, McRoberts (1990) has suggested accepting that one language will have official status everywhere — except in New Brunswick, which is roughly one-third francophone and, in fact, the only officially bilingual province. Some general trends in these regards may be noted from Tables 3 and 4.

Against this general background, it is interesting to document a *rise* in bilingualism; countrywide, it increased from 12% to 15% between 1961 and 1981 (see McRoberts, 1990). More complete figures are found in Table 5. Réjean Lachapelle, director of the demolinguistics division at Statistics Canada, saw the big increase in children's bilingualism (from 3% of English-mother-tongue speakers in 1971 to 11% in 1991) as due to immersion programmes — but this

Table 4 Assimilationist pressures on official-language minority-group speakers, by province, 1961 and 1986

Region	Minority mother tongue as % of population		Minority language at home as % of population	
	1961	1986	1961	1986
Newfoundland	0.7	0.5	0.4	0.4
Nova Scotia	5.4	4.1	3.5	2.9
New Brunswick	35.2	33.5	31.4	31.3
PEI	7.6	4.7	3.9	2.8
Quebec	13.3	10.4	14.7	12.3
Ontario	6.8	5.3	4.6	3.8
Manitoba	6.6	4.9	4.0	2.8
Saskatchewan	3.9	2.3	1.7	0.9
Alberta	3.2	2.4	1.4	1.1
British Columbia	1.6	1.6	0.5	0.6

Source: McRoberts (1990). Based upon 1961, 1971 and 1986 Statistics Canada census figures

Table 5 Official-language bilingualism

Region	1971	1981	1991
Quebec	28	33	36
New Brunswick	22	27	29
Ontario	9	11	12
Other Provinces	6	6	7
Canada as a whole	13	15	16

Note: Percentages for the 'other provinces' were quite similar; when a combined percentage was calculated for the western provinces (Manitoba, Saskatchewan, Alberta and British Columbia) and for the Atlantic provinces (Prince Edward Island, Newfoundland and Nova Scotia — excluding New Brunswick, of course), they were found to be identical.
Source: Statistcs Canada, and adaptation from Fraser (1993)

highlights the larger problem of how much bilingualism actually leads to more English–French exchange. For example, examination reveals that anglophone children schooled via immersion typically do not seem to make much *use* of their French competence (see Edwards, 1985). An even broader issue, of course, is the question of *level* of competence ascertainable from census findings (see Edwards, 1994b). As Whyte (1993) recently observed:

> Census-takers designate as bilingual anyone who claims to be able to carry on a conversation in both official languages. Statistics Canada found in a recent test that when people are asked if they can 'carry on a fairly long conversation on different topics,' there is a 'fairly significant decline' in bilinguals.

In any event, while policy — particularly educational policy — may have indeed resulted in census-assessed bilingualism increasing over the last 30 years or so, it is not by much; the territorial and polarised nature of Canadian bilingualism remains clear. It is ironic that French immersion programmes remain popular at the voluntary level while bilingualism-as-official-policy has hardly eliminated the 'two solitudes'. Kees de Bot has noted that 'for the outsider it is not easy to understand how a community can become less bilingual while a growing number of its members develop at least a fair command of both languages' (1994: 199). Perhaps the answers are above. Indeed, de Bot himself went on to muse on the findings that the 'products' of immersion hardly use French outside school.

A recent 'experiment' by Michel Vastel, writing in *L'actualité*, is perhaps suggestive; his experience is reported by Picard (1994a):

> He visits a bank a block away from the House of Commons and finds not a single French-speaking teller. A real-estate agent demands that he renounce the use of French in documents. The few francophones providing French-language services in provincial and municipal offices serve as mere translators for their bosses. Québécois movies are found in the 'foreign' section of the local video shop, and enrolling a child in a French-language school requires a six-month wait. 'Each time I hear "Sorry, I don't speak French", I wonder where they are, those graduates of immersion programs who are constantly telling us the English love us,' Mr Vastel writes.

This is reminiscent of another 'experiment', in which a francophone tested the government's promise of bilingual services in public transport; this was related by Mordecai Richler (1983):

> A Montreal friend of mine, though thoroughly bilingual, testily attempted to book a flight in French at the Toronto airport. But absolutely nobody at the Air Canada desk could speak the language. Finally, the help of a Dutch immigrant porter was enlisted and my friend was led onto the aeroplane grasping a form that declared the following disability: SPEAKS FRENCH ONLY (this example is also discussed by Reid, 1993, whose whole book is a catalogue of the vicissitudes of official bilingualism).

It is generally true that, as Gagnon states:

> The movement for bilingualism came from the top, but it cut deep into the Canadian psyche. Academics, the literati and Canadian nationalists were quick to realize that bilingualism was one of the features that distinguished Canada from its powerful neighbour to the south ... Total immersion

caught on like a bushfire ... Even the current disenchantment of the English-Canadian elite toward Quebec ... did not lower enrolment in immersion classes. In other words, learning French is not something you do because you're enthralled with Quebec ... You do it because learning French is politically useful, economically beneficial — and greatly enjoyable too. (Gagnon, 1993b)

Even though Gagnon has doubts about immersion education's lack of native-speaking teachers, and the subsequent effects upon children's French (see also Edwards, 1985), it *has* had the appeal noted above.

Immersion notwithstanding, the two official-language groups are, it would seem, increasingly isolated: the proportion of anglophones in Quebec and francophones elsewhere is falling. As Whyte (1993) notes, federal language policy has not disarmed Quebec nationalism or advanced the cause of state unity — as its creators had hoped it would. In several jurisdictions — Alberta, Saskatchewan and Quebec among them — the rights of official-language minority groups have been restricted and, it could be argued, this has occurred in response to federal policy. The general population is unsupportive of official bilingualism (in the West, perhaps 65% would like to see it scrapped). It seems clear enough that recent events have not made it more attractive to Canadians.

Multiculturalism

The Royal Commission on Bilingualism and Biculturalism also gave rise to the Canadian multiculturalism policy of 1971 (in 1988, a Multicultural Act was passed). Its aims were to assist cultural groups to develop and to contribute to society, to help them overcome any cultural barriers to mainstream participation, to promote 'creative encounters' and to assist in the learning of French and/or English. It is important to note that the policy was to be embedded in a *bilingual* (not multilingual) framework. If only the two 'charter' languages were to be emphasised, many wondered from the outset if some enduring difference between the status of the 'others' and that of the French and English was to be enshrined.

Official multiculturalism has also been seen as politically opportunistic in a country in which the 1981 Census revealed the following demographic break-down: 40% of British provenance, 27% French, 27% 'other'. Moreover, there has been sustained francophone criticism of the policy; the fear, above all, is that that community might somehow be reduced to the status of the 'others'. This fear has been strengthened in recent years by the falling fertility rate in Quebec. This now stands at 1.5 (overall, the Canadian rate is 1.8), and the 'replacement' rate is reckoned at 2.1 — hence, the Québécois can no longer even wield *la revanche du berceau.*

In any event, despite all the rhetoric about the Canadian 'mosaic' (as opposed to the American 'melting pot'), most commentators have agreed that, in both contexts, anglo-conformity has been the prevailing force (see Breton, 1986; Weinfeld, 1985; Wardhaugh, 1983). Raymond Breton (with Jeffrey Reitz) recently provided further insights here. In *The Illusion of Difference* (1994), they demon-strated that immigrant assimilation in Canada is essentially the same as in the

United States. (In fact, Americans are *more* likely than Canadians to endorse cultural retention; within Canada, those of British origins are more favourably disposed towards this retention than are other European-origin groups, and French-Canadians are the least favourable.) Canada is perhaps a more homogeneous (or more homogenising) society than is often thought (see *Globe & Mail*, 1994b).

Polls of attitudes towards multiculturalism generally confirm the findings of Breton & Reitz. There is a lack of awareness of the federal policy (for a start), lukewarm support for multiculturalism as an idea and a broad unwillingness to take positive *action*. There is, perhaps, support for the *symbolism* of multiculturalism (see Breton, 1986; Palmer, 1976).

At the moment, multiculturalism is being closely re-examined from both within and without the 'beneficiary' communities. While this cannot, I think, be attributed directly to the constitutional wrangling over the past dozen years, it is clear that, indirectly at least, the vigorous re-analysis of Canada-as-a-society, which has surfaced because of it, has meant that many federal institutions and policies have come under scrutiny. Certainly, the lukewarm and symbolic recognition of multiculturalism, the general tolerance for diversity unallied to any great desire for action, and doubts from within the 'other' communities about the value of a policy which stresses difference — these and other factors have only been accentuated recently.

The most basic debate, perhaps, is over the idea that by promoting diversity we can actually (and more democratically, it has been argued) promote unity. Reginald Bibby has recently suggested that, despite what seems to be an increasing public support for a 'melting pot', the multicultural policy *has* aided various groups to preserve aspects of their culture (the 'goodness' of this, itself, is of course contentious) and to better participate in the currents of Canadian life. But, he argues, the promotion of group *interaction* — in the interests of state unity — has been less successful (Bibby, 1990). Critics would say, of course, that this is precisely what a multicultural policy *cannot* do, because by its nature it stresses differences (many of which, for better or worse, are fairly trivial in nature: food fairs, dance festivals and the like).

Part of the problem with multicultural policy is that it also stresses collectivities rather than individuals. Canada, like other western democracies, has traditionally seen rights inhering in the latter rather than the former (though the stress here, obviously, can never be absolute; see also Edwards, in press-a). Perhaps, then, some of the public discontent can be viewed in this light. The apparently paradoxical findings of a federally-sponsored survey of attitudes, conducted by the Angus Reid Group (Canadian Press, 1991) — the first such broad survey in many years — can be better understood if this factor is taken into account. The poll found, for example, broad support (among a sample of over 3000 adults) for such 'multicultural' principles as the elimination of racism, the *recognition* of diversity and the promotion of equal job *access*, but less favourable views of policies seen to give some *groups* 'more than their fair share' (my italics). Similarly — perhaps based upon the unarticulated sense that supporting groups may mean supporting repugnant practices — respondents who would generally tolerate difference were unwilling to endorse such things as arranged marriages and cultural beliefs of male superiority. Beyond this, 46% thought that immigrants should be willing to adapt 'to be more like us' and 42% felt that Canadian unity was weakened by groups 'sticking to their old ways.'

In these views, Canadians seem not unlike other members of immigrant 'receiving' societies. Thus, for example, a very recent study from Australia (Ho et al., 1994) revealed 'considerable confusion over the policy of multiculturalism' (p. 69). Among a sample of 655 Australian-born residents of Darwin, strong support was found for services facilitating immigrant integration, and clear disapproval of those seen to 'favour migrants unfairly'. The analogy continues when we note, in Australia, the discrepancy between support for some basic multiculturalism principles and multicultural policy itself. The findings of Ho et al. also confirm earlier Australian work (e.g. the national survey of the Office of Multicultural Affairs, 1989).

Another Canadian poll (of 1800, by Ekos Research Associates and Anderson Strategic Research) found a hardening of attitudes towards immigrants, with about half feeling that unchecked immigration could fracture society and about one-third wanting immigrants who are more like Canadians (Canadian Press, 1992). Breton & Reitz (1994) have also reported that almost three-quarters of Canadians believe that immigrants who are unwilling to change their habits and attitudes often bring discriminatory practices upon themselves.

Some of the most important recent criticisms of official multiculturalism have come from within the 'ethnic' community. Thus, Neil Bissoondath (a writer, and nephew of V.S. Naipaul) has described federal policy as an 'opportunistic political' ploy, though not without a 'certain amount of heart and sincerity.' As it emphasises what is superficial, multiculturalism is seen to foster, at best, a benign and inactive tolerance; it ignores the deeper understanding that might have an ultimately consolidating influence. On the one hand, Bissoondath observes that, as policy:

> [If] the emphasis on federal bilingualism had seemed to favour franco-phone Quebec at the expense of the rest of the country, enhanced multiculturalism could be served up as a way of equalizing the political balance sheet. As René Lévesque once commented, 'Multiculturalism, really, is folklore. It is a "red herring". The notion was devised to obscure 'the Quebec business,' to give an impression that we are all ethnics and do not have to worry about special status for Quebec. (Bissoondath, 1993)

On the other hand, the lack of an overall vision of the nature of a multicultural society, the inability to reconcile diversity with unity, and the rushed and politicised nature of the federal policy all mean that whatever 'heart and sincerity' there may have been, have come to very little:

> [Multiculturalism] has highlighted our differences rather than diminished them, has heightened division rather than encouraged union. More than anything else, the policy has led to the institutionalization and enhance-ment of a ghetto mentality. And it is here that lies the multicultural problem as we experience it in Canada: a divisiveness so entrenched that we face a future of multiple solitudes with no central notion to bind us (Bissoondath,

1993; see also Breton & Reitz, 1994, on the report that minority-group members worry lest policies of pluralism marginalise them).

Bissoondath returned to the subject 18 months later (Makin, 1994). Acknowledging that the $25 million spent annually on official multicultural-policy activities is quite a small sum, he criticised the symbolism of multiculturalism. Clearly, his arguments — like those of other critics — do not reflect some blind rejection of diversity *per se*; rather, they are ones which question the government role. Bissoondath is of the opinion that 'any group worth its salt can finance its own lobbying and cultural events', that private efforts are appropriate for those wishing to retain ancestral languages, and so on.

I have, of course, stressed *criticisms* of multiculturalism here and it should be noted that not all minority-group members (or others) would endorse Bissoondath's views or those of 'mainstream' Canadians, as revealed in polls. But few would deny that, among other policies, multiculturalism is now under a more than usually powerful microscope. Furthermore, although it seems clear that matters of official bilingualism and multiculturalism, and matters of identity have been magnified because of recent political upheavals, it is also true that such issues are undergoing intense scrutiny throughout the world, especially (of course) in the 'receiving' societies. The allegedly divisive potential of multiculturalism has prompted several new books, dealing with such societies as Australia, the United States and Canada (see Edwards, in press-c). Indeed, it could be argued that concerns about diversity and discord, about group and individual rights, about pluralism and unity, are the major sociopolitical themes of our time. In many contexts and for many reasons a 'new order' is on the horizon (if only the mental horizon), and this inevitably means transition and the renegotiation of identity. Canadian crises, then, are a component of late twentieth-century identity politics.[3]

Monolingualism and Canadian Identity

In this final section, I want to deal briefly with the impact of recent events upon Canadian identity; many points, naturally, will already have been gleaned from the discussion so far. However, before turning to this broadest of issues, I also want to comment on the influence and power of a 'monolingual model' in Canada.

Perhaps this seems odd. After all, we have noted *increased* French–English bilingualism (although of a slight order) in the country. And, consider all the 'non-official' languages: the 1991 Census revealed that 430,000 people speak Chinese (at home, at least), 290,000 Italian, 150,000 Portuguese, 134,000 German and 50,000 Ukrainian. We can also, however, recall (on the one hand) the increasing polarisation of the French and English 'solitudes', the continuing shift to English among francophones outside Quebec, and the great non-use of French learned at school, and (on the other) the long-term instability of bilingualism involving the 'other' languages and the power of 'anglo-conformity'. Between the 1971 and 1991 Censuses, for example, some 425,000 speakers of Italian had dropped to the 290,000 noted above; German and Ukrainian speakers (in 1971) had numbered 215,000 and 145,000 respectively. Fold all these figures into broad public support for immigrants becoming 'more like us', the (at best) tepid endorsement of official bilingualism and multiculturalism, and (within Quebec) the rigorous attempts to solidify and protect French and to stream both newcomers and existing non-francophones more efficiently into *francophonie*. The result is a combination of 'natural' demographic and language-shift trends — abetted by the ever-increasing clout of English, worldwide — public perceptions of which side of the linguistic bread has the butter, and conscious policies, which would seem to imply a steady drift towards monolingualism or, at least, essentially monolingual functioning in most areas of public life.

This has been hastened by the hardening of views, on all sides, which has accompanied the Quebec–Canada altercations. If the promised Quebec referendum of 1995 fails, this is unlikely to mean a return to some pre-crisis linguistic and cultural *status quo*. If it succeeds, then I would expect even greater and more rapid growth of French and English monolingualisms. In a curious way, recent Canadian experience is supporting the old one-nation, one-language thesis, in contrast to the multicultural and multilingual pluralism which so many have been promoting as *the* scenario for tolerant democratic societies. There will, of course, continue to be a 'bilingual belt' between Quebec and the rest of the country — notably in parts of Ontario and, most strongly, in New Brunswick; however, the former is already under threat, and would likely be put even more at risk in a Canada *sans* Quebec. In New Brunswick — the only officially bilingual province, in which about one-third of the 700,000 inhabitants are francophone — bilingualism will endure longer but there, too, it is *already* under a pressure which can only increase.

The splitting-off of Quebec and the dismantling of official bilingualism in Canada which would likely ensue would remove the diglossic framework which, however shaky, has given *some* comfort to francophones outside Quebec. Support for the 'other' languages is likely to fall even below the low levels currently dependent upon official multiculturalism (provisions will still remain, no doubt, for immersion education and — more to the point here — for school language programmes for 'allophone' children: see the recent collection by Danesi, McLeod & Morris, 1993, for an overview of current provisions; and, within that collection, see Edwards, 1993). In a separate Quebec, of course, it is clear that the potency and position of French would be consciously and constantly supported.

Without Quebec, Canada would, in broad linguistic terms, come more closely to resemble Australia and, especially, the United States — countries in which, despite large numbers of non-English-speaking immigrants, the trend is inexorably away from multiple fluencies. I am certainly not endorsing this as a social good *per se*, but I am suggesting that there is, in many settings, a linguistic iron law: people will not maintain more than one language indefinitely if one serves them in all domains of importance. It seems to me that in a separated Canada the working out of this rule cannot but be expedited.

What then of Canadian identity, that perennial butterfly? Again, I think that we have reached a state in which, whatever the future, the *status quo* has gone forever. Political leaders, even those arguing strongly against Quebec separation, seem committed to a reworked federalism; some authors, as we have seen, have already presented conceptions of, and blueprints for, some new Canada (again, with or without Quebec). One could at the least argue, I suppose, that a Canada without Quebec would be more linguistically homogeneous, more overwhelmingly anglophone — and this *could* hasten the development of a Canadian identity. If official multiculturalism, in some form or other, also becomes part of a reworked federal landscape and if the present climate, in which the whole ethos of multiculturalism is being carefully scrutinised, persists — then this, too, could facilitate that development (as might the outright *dropping* of multiculturalism).

However, while a Quebec identity, already strong, would be further buttressed by independence, old obstacles to a Canadian identity would remain. These include, of course, the proximity to the broadly similar but much more expansive culture of the United States (within one hundred miles of whose borders most Canadians live), the strong regional loyalties in the country, and (relatedly) the unlikely geographical nature of Canada itself (which resembles Chile on its side). A post-Quebec Canada, faced with these factors, may well show the fissiparous tendencies — and the increased desire, in some quarters, to more closely associate with the United States — already outlined by some commentators.

In June 1991, *The Economist* published a special 'Survey on Canada', in which these matters were considered (see *Globe & Mail*, 1991). To overcome the many centrifugal forces affecting it, Canada needs a strong 'national ethic', for the present one appears 'decidedly frail' (the report noted). The multicultural policy and the general 'niceness' and 'tolerance' of Canadian society, the report continued, are hardly conducive to producing a general and binding fabric:

> Immigrants to Quebec … know what is expected of them, even if they do not like it: it is that they should become Quebeckers. That means that they should identify with Quebec's sense of history, its *projet de société* and its national ethic. Immigrants to the rest of Canada, however, are merely invited to learn English (it does not matter if they fail the simple test they are set after three years) and answer a few easy questions about Canada. They should also try to be nice.

What sort of country can be forged on the basis of what a former federal minister described as 'a community of communities'? And what does *The Economist* predict Canada might do to avoid disintegration? Like some latter-day Austria–Hungary: 'it will endeavour to make a virtue of its tolerance of decentralization' (this, it may be noted, is exactly what cultural pluralists would applaud). But this sort of 'policy', it is argued, is likely to eventually weaken the already fragile Canadian fabric: 'sooner or later Canadians are going to become Americans. Too bad.'

Is this a reasonable scenario or is it speculation of an extreme kind? The short answer is that no one can be sure — and this uncertainty about such hugely important matters is a measure of the current malaise, a malaise which undoubtedly predates the Quebec–Canada crises but has been, equally undoubtedly, exacerbated by them. When Andrew Coyne (1994) wrote recently that, in Canada, there was virtually nothing left to be loyal to, he evoked a predictably strong response. His basic points, however — the lack of 'animating principles' or 'conceptions of itself', the endless rearrangement of structure and symbol, and the constant controversy over 'basic axioms of nationhood' — have some substance. And, immediately following the election of the PQ in September 1994, Terrence Downey argued that, while Quebec nationalists clearly have a social vision, the rest of Canada lacks one, no longer has any 'national dream', no longer sees further than issues of money and commerce.

And yet, while one writer was complaining that 'the cultural ideal has become that of a hyphenated Canadian ... there is no cultural space for someone ... who wants to be a Canadian' (Valpy, 1994), a report from the 1991 Census revealed that more than three-quarters of a million people answered the question on ethnic origin by writing 'Canadian'. This number, refusing to say what culture their forebears came from, represents *more than a hundredfold increase* from the 69,000 who reported themselves as Canadian in the previous Census (1986: see Mitchell, 1993). Sociologists speculated that this massive increase was a sign of 'constitutional angst', that the Quebec crises had 'whipped up national fervour' (Quebec, unsurprisingly, had one of the lowest rates of reporting 'Canadian' ethnic origin). In the light of what has already been discussed, can we take this as a hopeful sign for an emerging national identity? Again, the answer is unclear.

The impression I want to leave, at the end, is one of great flux. Momentous things are happening in a Canada long regarded internationally as one of the blandest places on earth — but also as one of the most wealthy, tolerant, democratic and peaceful (indeed, a recent global ranking showed Canada to be the *best* of countries in overall 'quality-of-life' terms). If such a state is to splinter, it has been asked, what hope is there for other less fortunate countries? Yet Canada has also always been, socially and geographically, a rather unlikely country and it is possible, then, to ask instead how it has managed to cohere for so long. Whatever the outcome of this most recent and most bitter internal wrangling, there will — for good or ill — be lessons and insights of interest to many. Central among these is the incredibly powerful intertwining of language and culture with politics and statehood.

Notes

1. This concludes a very cursory review of material treated in my earlier papers. As in those papers, it will be seen in what follows that I have relied heavily upon the Toronto *Globe & Mail*, English Canada's 'national' newspaper. I have, however, used it more for 'factual' data than for 'editorial' information; in addition, I have referred to *francophone* reporters' pieces wherever possible. Information has also been gathered from, and checked with, the fortnightly reports of *Canadian News Facts*.
2. As with the first section, the following parts build upon earlier work and, consequently, omit various contextualising details.
3. A group of panellists (Bissoondath among them) was assembled for a CBC television programme examining multiculturalism and the question of 'who is a real Canadian.' While the usual arguments were made, for and against multiculturalism as idea and multiculturalism as policy, the timing of the programme (28 and 29 September 1994) is surely telling.

References

Bercuson, D. (1994) Building the will to rebuild. *Globe & Mail*, 13 September.
Bercuson, D. and Cooper, B. (1991) *Deconfederation: Canada Without Quebec*. Toronto: Key Porter.
Bibby, R. (1990) *Mosaic Madness*. Toronto: Stoddart.

Bissoondath, N. (1993) A question of belonging. *Globe & Mail*, 28 January.

Blohm, R. (1994) The bond market holds Quebec's fate. *Globe & Mail*, 9 August.

Breton, R. (1986) Multiculturalism and Canadian nation-building. In A. Cairns and C. Williams (eds) *The Politics of Gender, Ethnicity and Language in Canada*. Toronto: University of Toronto Press.

Breton, R. and Reitz, J. (1994) *The Illusion of Difference*. Toronto: C.D. Howe Institute.

Canadian Press (1991). Prejudice overshadows multiculturalism. *Chronicle Herald* (Halifax), 24 December.

— (1992) Survey showed immigrants unpopular. *Globe & Mail*, 14 September.

— (1994a) French on the decline in Montreal, study says. *Globe & Mail*, 30 March.

— (1944b) Film shows PQ candidate decrying native cultures. *Globe & Mail*, 6 August.

Cernetig, M. (1994) Klein calls on Westerners to unite. *Globe & Mail*, 26 May.

Cloutier, E., Gay, J. and Latouche, D. (1992) *Le Virage*. Montreal: Québec–Amérique.

Cook, R. (1994) Letter. *Globe & Mail*, 17 September.

Coyne, A. (1994) Where nothing means anything, what's left to be loyal to? *Globe & Mail*, 6 June.

Danesi, M., McLeod, K. and Morris, S. (eds) (1993) *Heritage Languages and Education*. Oakville, Ontario: Mosaic.

Davidson, J. (1994) Separatism's costs widespread. *Globe & Mail*, 10 June.

de Bot, K. (1994) Comment. *International Journal of the Sociology of Language* 110, 193–201.

Delacourt, S. (1994) Quebec land not inviolable, PM says. *Globe & Mail*, 25 May.

Dion, S. (1992) Explaining Quebec nationalism. In R. Weaver (ed.) *The Collapse of Canada?* Washington: Brookings Institution.

Downey, T. (1994) What does Canada want, beyond money and trade? *Globe & Mail*, 15 September.

Edwards, J. (1985) *Language, Society and Identity*. Oxford: Blackwell

— (1993) Identity and language in the Canadian educational context. In M. Danesi, K. McLeod and S. Morris (eds) *Heritage Languages and Education*. Oakville, Ontario: Mosaic.

— (1994a) Language policy and planning in Canada. *Annual Review of Applied Linguistics* 14, 126–36.

— (1994b) *Multilingualism*. London & New York: Routledge.

— (in press-a) Ethnolinguistic pluralism and its discontents: A Canadian study and some general observations. *International Journal of the Sociology of Language*.

— (in press-b) The power of nationalism: The Canadian referendum of 1992. In W. Fase (ed.) *Proceedings of the Second International Conference on the Maintenance and Loss of Minority Languages*. Amsterdam: Swets & Zeitlinger.

— (in press-c) Complaints of our time, or, finding the middle ground. *Journal of Multilingual and Multicultural Development*.

Fortier, D. (1985) *Annual Report: Commissioner of Official Languages*. Ottawa: Supply & Services Canada.

Fraser, G. (1993) Bilingualism grows across Canada. *Globe & Mail*, 13 January.

Gagnon, L. (1993a) Bloc Québécois distances itself from Parizeau election musings. *Globe & Mail*, 23 January.

— (1993b) Bilingualism cuts deeply into the Canadian psyche. *Globe & Mail*, 10 April.

— (1993c) More doubts about the benefits of French immersion. *Globe & Mail*, 17 April.

— (1994a) Contrary to its reputation, Quebec gives natives a fairer shake. *Globe & Mail*, 9 April.

— (1994b) Why De Gaulle uttered those rousing, contentious words in 1967. *Globe & Mail*, 21 May.

— (1994c) The West should keep calm and let Quebec go about its business. *Globe & Mail*, 28 May.

— (1994d) For ardent separatists, the referendum is the last chance. *Globe & Mail*, 3 September.

Gibson, G. (1994) *Plan B: The Future of the Rest of Canada*. Vancouver: Fraser Institute.

Globe & Mail (1991) *The Economist: Survey of Canada*. 19 July.

— (1993) Separation would do Canada no great harm. Reprinted editorial from *The Economist*, 1 November.

— (1994a) Time to be honest about Quebec. 20 May.

— (1994b) The myth of Canadian diversity. 13 June.

Héroux, M. (1990) *The Office of the Commissioner of Official Languages: A Twenty-Year Chronicle from 1970 to Mid-1989*. Ottawa: Supply & Services Canada.

Ho, R., Niles, S., Penney, R. and Thomas, A. (1994) Migrants and multiculturalism: A survey of attitudes in Darwin. *Australian Psychologist* 29, 62–70.

Koring, P. (1994a) Quebec inviolable, Bouchard says. *Globe & Mail*, 19 May.

— (1994b) Bouchard forecasting rain on parade. *Globe & Mail*, 20 May.

— (1994c) Call us when it's over, M. Bouchard. *Globe & Mail*, 21 May.

Lamont, L. (1994) *Breakup: The Coming End of Canada and the Stakes for America*. Toronto: Penguin.

Lisée, J.-F. (1994) *Le Tricheur: Robert Bourassa et les Québécois*. Montreal: Boréal.

Little, B. (1994) Study bleak on referendum. *Globe & Mail*, 10 June.

Mackie, R. (1994a) Sovereignty, separatism ring different bells. *Globe & Mail*, 10 March.

— (1994b) PQ prints magazine on plans for future. *Globe & Mail*, 28 March.

— (1994c) Anglos launch drive for jobs. *Globe & Mail*, 18 April.

— (1994d) 50% see win as mission nod for PQ. *Globe & Mail*, 15 July.

— (1994e) Sovereignty support slipping while PQ in front, poll says. *Globe & Mail*, 16 July.

— (1994f) Johnson steps up attack on separatists. *Globe & Mail*, 30 July.

Makin, K. (1994) How Canadians' roots become ethnic walls. *Globe & Mail*, 27 June.

McKenna, B. (1993) Power shifts at Quebec Inc. *Globe & Mail*, 3 November.

McRoberts, K. (1990) Federalism and political community. *Globe & Mail*, 19 March to 2 April.

McRoberts, K. and Monahan, P. (eds) (1993) *The Charlottetown Accord, the Referendum, and the Future of Canada*. Toronto: University of Toronto Press.

Mitchell, A. (1993) Huge number Canadian and nothing else. *Globe & Mail*, 24 February.

Monahan, P. (1994) International law isn't on Mr Parizeau's side. *Globe & Mail*, 19 May.

Nelde, P., Labrie, N. and Williams, C. (1992) The principles of territoriality and personality in the solution of linguistic conflicts. *Journal of Multilingual and Multicultural Development* 13, 387–406.

Office of Multicultural Affairs (1989). *Issues in Multicultural Australia, 1988*. Canberra: Australian Government Publishing Service.

Palmer, H. (1976) Reluctant hosts. In Report of the Second Canadian Conference on Multiculturalism, *Multiculturalism as State Policy*. Ottawa: Supply & Services Canada.

Picard, A. (1993a) Quebec nationalists take aim at new language legislation. *Globe & Mail*, 8 May.

— (1993b) Language bill called betrayal. *Globe & Mail*, 15 May.

— (1993c) Separatism outshouts federalism in Quebec. *Globe & Mail*, 26 October.

— (1994a) Québécois voices. *Globe & Mail*, 31 March.

— (1994b) Playing with fire for federation. *Globe & Mail*, 16 June.

— (1994c) Trail notes. *Globe & Mail*, 9 August.

Reid, S. (1993) *Lament for a Notion*. Vancouver: Arsenal Pulp.

Resnick, P. (1991) *Toward a Canada–Quebec Union*. Montreal: McGill-Queen's University Press.

— (1994) *Thinking English Canada*. Toronto: Stoddart.

Richler, M. (1983) Quebec: Language problems. *Atlantic*, June, 10–24.

— (1991) A reporter at large. *New Yorker*, 23 September, 40–92.

— (1992) *Oh Canada! Oh Quebec!* Toronto: Penguin.

— (1994) O Quebec. *New Yorker*, 30 May, 50–7.

Séguin, R. (1993a) PQ predicts independent Quebec by 1995. *Globe & Mail*, 25 January.

— (1993b) Integration tied into Bill 101. *Globe & Mail*, 15 February.

— (1993c) Sign law violates rights, UN says. *Globe & Mail*, 22 April.

— (1993d) Ad campaign aims to mobilize opinion against language bill. *Globe & Mail*, 2 June.

— (1993e) Quebec self-rule assured, BQ says. *Globe & Mail*, 27 October.

Simpson, J. (1991) If it left, would everything be all right? Review of Bercuson and Cooper *Deconfederation: Canada without Quebec. Globe & Mail*, 24 August.
— (1993) *Faultlines*. Toronto: Harper Collins.
Taylor, C. (1993) *Reconciling the Solitudes*. Montreal: McGill-Queen's University Press.
Valpy, M. (1994) Coming home. *Globe & Mail*, 2 July.
Wardhaugh, R. (1983) *Language and Nationhood*. Vancouver: New Star.
Weinfeld, M. (1985) Myth and reality in the Canadian mosaic. In R. Bienvenue and J. Goldstein (eds) *Ethnicity and Ethnic Relations in Canada*. Toronto: Butterworths.
Whyte, K. (1993) Official bilingualism has failed to achieve its true purposes. *Globe & Mail*, 8 May.
Winsor, H. (1994a) Support for PQ defies logic. *Globe & Mail*, 13 August.
— (1994b) Many may point at wrong villain. *Globe & Mail*, 13 September.
York, G. (1994) Bouchard's stand on natives clashes with advisor's opinion. *Globe & Mail*, 27 May.

The Debate

Push–Pull Factors: The Importance of Economics

Dennis Ager (Aston University): One of your concerns in this paper is the economic viability of Quebec as a separate state, and whether or not it would be possible for a future state to exist where a nation — or a region or a grouping of people — currently exists. Something which I feel is of importance here is the question of *attraction*, the economic pull of language shift. It is well established in the research that the major determinant in language shift is economics — if using your mother tongue excludes you from the workplace, then you drop your language to get a job. This happens, no matter what you may feel about group identity. Clearly, one of the main supports for the existence of an independent Quebec and the vibrant group identity which exists in the province has been the fact that you can actually work through the medium of French in commerce and industry. The possibility for people to retain an economic activity within French is a fundamental feature of Quebec nationalism and the attractiveness to individuals of this potential state. I think it's the economic pull factor for individuals which is one of the driving forces of French separatism — as much as any collective feeling that there is an economically viable future.

John Edwards: It's true, I didn't talk about economics in that sense here, although I do elsewhere. People are motivated strongly by economic, or perhaps more broadly, pragmatic considerations and, as you say, that's obviously a recurring feature. But I think in some cases, one can go too far. I've been accused myself on occasion of suggesting a very simple-minded economic reductionism and of course it is not that simple. But the fact remains that if you can't earn your living and if you can't see your kids making a living if you keep to your first language, that's a powerful, powerful motivation for shifting language.

And that, of course, is one of the other great imponderables in this situation in Canada, because even the most fervent nationalists would admit that there's no particular guarantee that they're going to be better off economically in French, just because they'll become a separate state. After all, much of their trading situation will remain exactly the same; they'll still be just six million Francophones in the North American sea, which is 40 times larger. But, nonetheless, I think they feel that if they institutionalise things in a certain way, if they capitalise on the way French speakers have taken control of the reins of economic power, then perhaps the economic viability of their future is more secure. But it is an imponderable, certainly.

Lewis Glinert (SOAS, University of London): It is important, at least in principle, to distinguish between the economic concerns of the individual and the state, because the state is, after all, able to allow itself the license to buck economic trends, the individual, less so. I wonder at what point on this scale do economic concerns become absolutely paramount. For example, at the level of local government? And at what point do people making policies begin to behave like individuals?

Sue Wright (Aston University): Once you focus on economic arguments, the case for monolingualism is quite strong at all levels. Presumably, there is now less money spent in Quebec on language-associated costs than in the past, because things are only in the one language. You don't need a translation; you don't need two versions.

John Edwards: I'm not sure what the current situation is. I think at the level of the Assemblée Nationale, they still produce documents in English, but perhaps not all of them as would have been the case before.

As to the overall cost effect, perhaps there has been some financial benefit gained from the move from bilingualism to monolingualism, but, on the other hand, there has been a great increase in other linguistic activity with high costs — in the area of French terminology, for example.

Keith Watson (University of Reading): Presumably, in Canada as a whole, *Kellogg's* and all the others who produce everything in two languages would be only too delighted, if Quebec seceded, to revert to English.

John Edwards: I think a post-separation Canada would probably jettison, in fairly short order, official bilingualism.

Lee Rotherham (Birmingham University): Surely, we should look at this the other way round. Haven't economic factors come to the fore because nationalism, regionalism, whatever we call it, has been successful? French-Canadians have achieved success in cultural and linguistic terms and now that those concerns are less prominent than when English was the dominant and encroaching language, economic concerns have come to the fore.

Dennis Ager: Then you are suggesting that economic factors are secondary and that group identity and solidarity win out over personal advantage. I'm not convinced and I don't think the statistics on language shift in a number of situations — both past and present — will bear you out.

Srikant Sarangi (University of Wales — Cardiff): I do agree that economics is a very powerful motivational force. This is not just so in the case of the individual who makes choices but it is also a powerful tool for manipulating groups. The language of economics is what politicians bring into play when other elements such as the political, or the cultural, or the linguistic fail. This is precisely what has happened in the recent referenda on Europe. The debate in Sweden about joining the European Union was all about employment. And it seems to me that this is happening everywhere in public life; even quality of life is always referred to in economic terms. It is part of the dominant discourse.

Linda Thompson (University of Durham): You painted a picture of Canada as internationally wealthy, tolerant, democratic, peaceful, the best overall quality of life in the world. I'm just wondering what would happen if economic conditions were to change as they have in other countries, and I'm drawing a parallel with what has happened here in Britain since the 1980s. We've seen a less accommodating attitude emerging towards groups different from ourselves; we've seen the British Nationalist Party elected to office; we've seen a number of changes which we wouldn't perhaps have expected to see, because of changes in economic circumstances nationally. I'm just wondering what would happen to attitudes in Canada if economic conditions change and become less favourable.

John Edwards: Well, it has already happened. Canada has a terrible debt problem and this has led to predictable responses in the areas you're most concerned with. A certain part of the appeal of the Reform Party has been the argument that bilingual programmes cannot be justified in the current economic situation. I think in some sense — I want to stress, parenthetically, that I'm not in favour in any way of the Reform Party philosophy — that when times are good, you do find a broader tolerance for policies which are, let's say, of a cultural nature and they are often the first to go when times get tougher, because you can't show a clear association between what you invest and what you get back. And this has been incorporated into the larger debate about Canadian identity. 'Why should we pay people to remain separate?' 'Should the Canadian government be in the business of encouraging people to think of themselves in some "hyphenated" way?' That's the level of rhetoric which you often hear expressed. In fact, Canada doesn't spend a lot of money on multiculturalism and very little on these 'trivial' linguistic manifestations, but still the perception is that — particularly when times are tough, when we're trying to forge an identity, when we're trying to deal with the two warring charter groups — it doesn't make sense to pay for these things.

Deirdre Martin (Birmingham University): Certain economic arguments appeal to different classes within society. I was wondering whether in Quebec, there has been a class analysis of attitudes towards the economic situation of Quebec or towards being monolingual? There are groups here that would see themselves as advantaged in a mythical white-only Britain and so certain political and economic arguments appeal to them. Are there similar groups in Quebec?

John Edwards: Well, the elites in Quebec — whether or not they're federalist-minded liberals or members of the Bloc québécois — already have a very good command of both languages, so bilingualism is not a problem for them. It may be for other groups. However, the argument has been made that an independent, monolingual Quebec might actually disadvantage ordinary citizens by denying them access to the bilingualism that permits access to the rest of North America.

There have been a couple of French language treatments of class issues, but I don't think they're very satisfactory quite frankly, because they hearken back to a very old-fashioned, rigid, Marxist view of things and I don't think it accords with reality. It is, of course, a very difficult area. Quebec society is in such a state of flux: the so-called quiet revolution was just yesterday; the control of the Catholic Church was there until just yesterday; the Anglophones were in the key economic positions just yesterday. Everything is moving and, perhaps for this reason, the Quebec electorate is tending to draw back from crossing the line to full independence. Even among people who are generally sympathetic to the nationalist cause, who are willing to believe that yes, an independent Quebec might be good for them, there is a feeling that so many things have happened so fast that they can't be asked to sign on the dotted line just yet.

Deirdre Martin (Birmingham University): So there isn't a group within Quebec which sees itself as being sold an argument that its members will be economically better off, there will be more jobs for them — that isn't used as a line by the nationalists?

John Edwards: Perhaps, but, as far as I can see, it hasn't been broken down between the different strata of society. The general line that is being peddled is that everyone will be better off in an independent Quebec. We have the resources, we have the people and so on to be a nation state. But I'm suggesting that it hasn't been targeted more precisely than that because it's really too early.

Stephen Barbour (University of Middlesex): No doubt we'll keep returning to the point I'm going to make, but it seems crucial here. We all know that when politicians and others use the terms 'nation', 'nation state', they are often promoting the belief that the economic unit, the linguistic-cultural unit and the political unit should coincide. Which, of course, is what is happening in Quebec. We all know that this is a great distortion, because in case after case after case, they don't coincide. If we look at Quebec, there are good arguments for saying that at many levels the economic unit that people are operating in is North America, or the world if you like, because there's a much stronger economic link between Quebec and New York than between Quebec and British Columbia. So the economic unit is not Quebec and it's probably not Canada either. The linguistic-cultural unit was, until relatively modern times, Francophone Canada, which was of course concentrated in Quebec, but with many other Francophone groups in neighbouring provinces. Neither of these units could be — or had any possibility of being — a nation state. The political creation of a Quebec nation state would leave out the other Francophone Canadians and it still wouldn't be the economic unit. I think this confusion which politicians propagate, this belief that there can be this coincidence between the economic, the political and the linguistic-cultural is a major cause of problems. Here it is a mirage.

Sue Wright: If I sum up what we've said so far, I think that a number of us are tending to agree that language loyalty is linked as closely, if not more so, to economic advantage than to feelings of solidarity. This has profound implications for all our discussions on group identity.

Questions of Identity

John Rex (University of Warwick): Part of my job in life is to be concerned with definitions. I'm concerned with what I call infantile ethnicity, I'm concerned with *ethnies*, ethnic nationalism, the modernising nation, empires, post-imperial nationalism, immigrant and migrant transnational ethnic communities and so on. All of these terms require precise definition. Some of them come apart in your hands when you use them. But the most slippery term of all is 'identity'. Let me say some of the things I think about the usage of this term. Firstly, one way of over-simplifying it is to say that it answers the question: 'What am I?' The prior question to that is 'Am I?' — which is a psychological question, about whether the individual has a sense of self as a subject to cope with the world — and there is a whole psychological literature dealing with that. The next question is 'Who am I?' or 'What am I?' in the sense of 'To what group do I belong?' Now, our answer is that most human beings learn at quite simple levels of society to live with multiple identities — and these become ever more complex in more complex societies. But everybody has one particular identity among all the others which gives them a particular 'buzz', which takes them back to 'mother's breast' and sacredness and so on. And so we have to ask the question, 'Is it when you're with people who speak the same language as you that you get that kind of "buzz"?' This is possibly true; so being with your own linguistic group is important for identity. Being out of it is harder for the individual. Would anybody dispute such a claim?

It's when we look at the linguistic community as a whole, that problems arise for group identity, because language overspills groups. Francophone Canada is — and was — much bigger than Quebec, but there has been a hijacking of the language question by Quebec nationalism and all of the other Francophone Canadians are left out of the deal.

Another facet of identity which probably confuses the issue isn't about this group that gives a 'buzz', it's really concerned with what is termed the cognitive mapping of the world. The individual asks, 'What social objects are in the world, including that one that is called me?' And the answer to this may be in political or legal terms. Now when people are talking about identity they're sometimes talking about that. I would just urge us to be precise when speaking about identity.

And a last point. Membership, the thrilling membership of the group that gives you that nice kind of 'buzz' is perhaps less important than we make it out to be. People sometimes suggest that it's the most important dynamic in politics today and I don't think it is.

John Edwards: The idea of multiple identities is a very common concept and it's equally true that one has to be precise and define which particular identity one is talking about. Here, of course, I'm talking about ethnic or ethno-linguistic identity which is not the only identity that's possible, but it is the one which can be most easily manipulated in the current context.

Stephen Barbour: I agree, too, that multiple identities are what most of us have. Where I think the problem arises is when the unity of the nation is given special, almost sacred, importance. This causes endless problems, particularly when the concepts of nation and nation state are conflated. It means, for example, that if the nation we're talking about today is Canada, the Anglophones in Quebec, who, in their daily lives, must regularly have the experience of being a minority, can't be treated as such, because they are not a minority within the Canadian nation state. So this sacredness of the nation causes all sorts of distortions.

Sue Wright: There is no problem with multiple identities if no single allegiance has to be exclusive. When total commitment to one identity is required then there are conflicts. To cite the European Union again, this is precisely the position of the various nationalist groups — the inability to admit that there can be layers of allegiance — to the region, the nation, the supra-state. Surely, in the present case, there must be numerous Quebeckers who are quite happy to be Quebecker, Canadian and North American. They will add on to that language, religion, profession, sex etc.

John Edwards: Of course. And regional loyalties are particularly strong in Canada. One of the things which is not sufficiently appreciated is that in many ways Canada is a very unlikely country, strung out over a wide geographical area. Canadians may be able to forge a sense of identity in relatively adverse conditions or when they meet on some other ground. But, in the main, there are Newfoundlanders, there are Nova Scotians and so on. I'm not saying that these people don't have the sense of an over-arching state — they do. But it is actually very hard to find markers which differentiate Anglophone Canadians from Americans. It is a very real problem for the creation of any specifically national identity, when 80–90% of your population lives within 100 miles of this giant.

Nik Coupland (University of Wales — Cardiff): Perhaps we should consider issues of methodology in studying identity. I think we have reason to worry about what sort of contribution linguistics has made to the discussion we're having and in fact general discussions of identity. From a linguistic point of view, it strikes me that there are two traditions at work which you could possibly entertain, which could begin to make some progress on the question of forming identity. I can't speak on the Canadian context at all, and in fact the background to the work I'm currently doing and to which I can refer is the situation in Wales.

The two traditions might be these: on the one hand, you might give up on the seemingly impossible task of accessing identity as a construct directly, and then you might fall back on studying the area through various sorts of linguistic analysis — the identificational work that people do. So I think perhaps through critical discourse analysis, one could gain access to the way in which identity is made resonant, either one's own identity or other groups' identities in various situations. This is an approach I've used, not in the study of ethnic identity, but in the study of age-related identity. On the other hand, as a linguist, one might make some progress by attempting to deconstruct what I would say is the rather simplistic association between a language and an identity, and perhaps begin to see a language more as a cluster of varieties, as a cluster of symbolic potentials and identify the particular identity consequences of using a particular variety of language. I think that either of those approaches has an input to make.

John Edwards: I fully agree that we need more and different ways of approaching the study of identity, if only because of the obvious virtues of triangulation. In Social Psychology, one of the latest thrusts is towards discourse analysis and what it can tell us. So, rather than going up to people and asking them what they are, we can now approach it in a more subtle way.

John Rex: I think what Nik Coupland was saying was that you seem to regard language as a fixed thing which people attach themselves to. There is a similar type of argument concerning ethnicity. But obviously ethnicity and language are much more flexible things.

John Edwards: I've focused on language and identity here because it's such an obvious feature of the Canadian context. But you can find other contexts, where people want to argue very strongly for a sense of distinctiveness that need not be allied to language — and I've talked about this at length in my book, *Language, Society and Identity*.

Nik Coupland: In the work that Peter Garrett and I have been involved in, we have found that if, by various means, you get as close as possible to the sorts of identificational work that people are prepared to do outside of the traditional questionnaire or matched guise studies and so on, then you end up with a picture of identity which is very complex, but which is not impossibly complex. The notion of Welshness revealed in our data is but one of a set of dimensions that people routinely appeal to in order to characterise themselves and their neighbours, variably across contexts. So Welshness should be seen in conjunction with other very familiar social-psychological dimensions such as status, confidence, likeableness, authenticity in ways in which, through more detailed study, we can begin to latch on to. And this will take us away from the simplistic association between a language label and something which we consider as social identity.

John Edwards: I don't think so much that it's simplistic, although of course some handlings of it may well be. I do think that it's a different level of organisation of the subject. For example, there's a great deal more complexity about French–English relations at the moment in Canada than what I've said. Nonetheless, I think it's quite justifiable when you're working at some sort of macro-political level to say that this is the package we have to make sense of — while not being unaware that there are all sorts of details at work. I think very often that's exactly the level which most people respond to and which most politicians and political parties use. It's not so much that it's a simplistic dimension, it's a question of what's appropriate. It's an interesting division between the individual as complex individual and the individual buying into one or two simplistic labels to be in the group.

Nik Coupland: It could also be worthwhile to study how the association between a language label and this notion of identity is rendered simplistic by discursive work done in other settings, for example through the media. I think the danger is that, as sociolinguists, we follow the end product of those discursive practices rather than trying to unpack them.

Lewis Glinert (SOAS University of London): You said earlier that Anglophone Canada has difficulty in searching for its identity. I'm a bit puzzled about this, trying to fit it into the perspective of Frederik Barth, the Norwegian anthropologist, who suggested, very influentially, that boundary markers are more important than cultural difference. In other words, the wish to differentiate oneself is actually more important than the content of the culture. If one says that the Canadians do want to be what they are, because they are not what Americans are, then one is left thinking, surely they must have enough symbols at their disposal to create that differentiation. Or is there something more than Barth's theory at work here?

John Edwards: No, on the contrary, I think Barth's theory applies here. The idea of continuity in group boundaries even though the cultural 'stuff' within them can change over time is very useful. It's just that people will ask themselves what the cultural content is at the moment, and Canadians have always had a lot of trouble agreeing on that. At the moment the problem is double-edged — the influence from the south of which we've spoken and then the fact that a lot of things have changed recently, for example, the bringing back of the constitution, which only happened 10 or 12 years ago. The pull of the US and the awareness of being in a state of flux both feed into this boundary maintenance.

Srikant Sarangi (University of Wales, Cardiff): I wonder whether multiple identities are possible in the Quebeckers' situation. They can look at themselves in terms of multiple identities, but it is one identity which is played to a particular tune at a particular time. It comes down to one particular identity which has become very important in a particular struggle. Multiple identity is fine as a concept, but it doesn't work in practice.

John Edwards: No, I disagree. It does work in practice. We do wear different hats depending on the context. What we're arguing about on some occasions is which particular hat we ought to be wearing in order to engage in a debate, which hat we have been given to wear, which hat we have been told we ought to be wearing. An example, in the Canadian context, is the serious consideration of greater formal provisions for aboriginal self-government, although nobody knows what form this will take. Again, a lot of this discussion was predicated on the idea of a particular identity being brought to the fore, in a collectivist sense — First Nations, first 'ethnicities'. The idea seemed to be progressing, attracting a lot of goodwill, but in the middle of this debate, a group of aboriginal women put up their hands and said, 'Wait a minute, you're asking us to discuss these matters at a certain level and it's not a level that we're particularly keen on. If you grant rights on a collectivist basis, you may actually be disadvantaging us, because you may be perpetuating a system, many elements of which we don't care for very much.' So this group within a group was in the interesting position of appealing to the federal government on the basis of the Charter of Rights and Freedoms, and these women were saying they would rather be treated in the individual sense of the Charter, than on a collectivist basis. This created something of a stir, because it was a sharp reminder that people should not just assume that there is only one level the debate could take place at — group talking to group. These people reminded us that groups are not monolithic.

Sue Wright: Isn't this a difference too between the Anglo-Saxon tradition and the French tradition, both of which Canada has inherited? The French state won't treat with groups, only with the individual. Even the mild and timorous efforts of the British in the area of multiculturalism have been termed 'ghettoisation' by some French commentators.

John Edwards: Yes, this idea of individual rights has been a tendency in Western democracies for the last couple of hundred years. They've never been able to achieve it completely, nor, you might argue, ought they to. But it's always been seen as a safeguard against the very thing these aboriginal women complained about.

Lee Rotherham: I'd like to add something on this question of the fundamental difference between the French-Canadian concept and the English-Canadian concept of nation. This was particularly evident at the time of the founding of the Royal Commission on Bilingualism in 1963, because the first problem it had was the definition of what its members were actually investigating, and they came to the conclusion that they had to translate the English-Canadian concept with the word 'nation' and the French-Canadian one with the French word 'race'. The

English-Canadians saw Canada — the French-Canadians, the linguistic group — as the nation. So there's actually a very different perception between the two.

John Edwards: I wouldn't put it that way myself. I don't think it's a question of the actual perception being different — I just think the Anglo-Canadian mind never had to focus on the issue, and it made blanket assumptions that this is essentially an Anglophone country. It didn't spend much time examining these questions; it didn't have to perhaps; now it has been forced to. The Quebec experience was, of course, different from the beginning. It's quite clear where that particular heritage came from. So I don't think that if you had questioned people closely that you would have discovered great differences in what constitutes their idea of a nation. It's just that one group had to think about it and had to spend a lot of time thinking about it and the other group didn't.

Sue Wright: Dominant monolingual blindness!

John Edwards: Yes, indeed.

Guy Snaith (University of Liverpool): Language use is actually quite revealing and tends to support what Lee was saying. For example, all the English-Canadian provinces have provincial parliaments whereas in Quebec you get the Assemblée Nationale. When you're doing research you go to the *National* Library of Canada in Ottawa, and to the Bibliothèque *nationale* du Québec in Montreal — how can you have two national libraries in one country? This causes English-Canadians to query the Quebeckers' use of the term 'nation'. They perceive Quebec as a 'province', just 'part of the nation'. But, in the choice of the term 'national' for institutions in Quebec, the Quebeckers are saying, 'We are a nation'.

Helen Kelly-Holmes (Aston University): Nobody has mentioned the other groups in this equation. What about the First Nations and immigrant groups? What are their feelings about an independent Quebec? Do they stand to win or lose?

John Edwards: The growth of the social and political clout of the allophone groups, who now, collectively, number as many as the Francophones, has been very important . They're now saying that, although originally there may have been two charter groups, this myth doesn't serve anymore and that they are not willing to live in a country which defines itself in that way.

Lee Rotherham: I wonder, John, do you think that the far north of Quebec is a key variable in the independence argument? Does Quebec think it can go it alone with the northern resources intact?

John Edwards: I think so, and I think that's why the Quebec nationalist leaders have been so keen at every opportunity to say that Quebec can't be divided up and why they are so unwilling to make any territorial claims in favour of aboriginal groups. This is precisely because the economists who are favourable to their cause are telling them that they have a rich resources base. For example, they sell a large amount of hydro-electric power to the Americans. It's pretty clear that an independent Quebec would have to have fairly good and open access to these resources in order to remain viable, so the Quebeckers are unlikely to compromise in any way.

Peter Noble (University of Reading): Earlier, when you were talking about there being a general feeling of goodwill towards aboriginal groups and the calls for greater autonomy, I did think that we should have distinguished between Anglophone Canada and Francophone Canada. My impression, when I was in Montreal in 1993, was that there was still considerable resentment over the Oka incidents, that there was considerable feeling over water rights and hunting rights in Northern Quebec. Sympathy, even among very sophisticated Francophones in Montreal and Quebec City, was limited on this question, which ties in with what you were actually saying in your paper, about the distinction between the attitudes of the two communities, Anglophone and Francophone. This is a new development because the Francophones always prided themselves, looking back over their history, that their relations with the First Nations had been better than the English-speaking communities.

John Edwards: Well, I think it's mentioned in the paper that one of the things that feeds into the greater Francophone intolerance towards aboriginal demands is that there is a clash of nationalisms at work in Canada and energies can't be diluted in that way, if one is going to look after one's own group. There is more than one group which feels itself dominated by Anglo-Canada. On the other hand, you may have noticed a report by Bissoondath, cited in the paper, which pointed out that in recent times, aboriginal groups in Quebec have actually been treated better than they have in Anglo-Canada in terms of opportunities for language retention, some degree of autonomy in the sphere of education and so on. But again, all this has to be put against the background, that no matter how good the treatment may have been in some areas, it's generally been pretty lousy. There's nothing much to be proud of, anywhere, across the board. Nor do I think there's any great reason to imagine that the tide is going to change significantly for aboriginal groups. There is a feeling that these people have been very badly treated, but essentially they remain powerless groups and they're not likely to be able to exact significant changes in their condition.

Peter Noble: Yes, but what I was saying was that the goodwill was not equal.

John Edwards: It's quite true that it's uneven, but it's not clear that the situation is worse in Francophone Quebec. It's different, and I wouldn't want anyone to lose sight of the fact that the general level of treatment has been shameful.

Helen Kelly-Holmes: What about those Francophones living outside Quebec? How are they regarded by the Quebeckers and how do they define their identity? Is it on a regional or linguistic basis?

John Edwards: Well, yes you do have the Fransaskoise and the Franco-Ontarians and it's quite true that they have a regional sense — a sense of place. But they also look back to Quebec as a source and they have a great interest in the debate in terms of how it's going to affect them.

Julian Edge (Aston University): While I wouldn't want to dispute the analysis so far, I find it slightly dispiriting that there is no identity in the Canadian situation which accepts these old-world tensions, but says that our identity is always in the sense of becoming what we are becoming, as we live with these tensions, and our identity is emergent in this situation. It's not only a question of acknowledging potential multiple identities, but also the necessarily hybrid identity which arises from being involved here, now, in these times with these histories. Or is that really just not an issue?

John Edwards: On the contrary, that is in fact the issue. You could phrase it in terms of whether people are satisfied with that sense of who they are or whether they want to move on to something a little firmer.

Julian Edge: I wonder if the idea of that 'firm' identity somehow existing at a paradigmatic level is part of the problem — these old world concepts of identity, are we one of these, or one of those?

John Edwards: It may well be an old-world problem, a product of nineteenth century nationalism, I wouldn't dispute you on that, but it's nonetheless the way many people think. It's a particular problem for so-called receiving societies, where there is wave after wave of new people, changing the scene all the time. You don't have a closed system in which a stable group works out its problems; the system is porous. For example, in Quebec, faced with the declining birth-rate, fears for the survival of French and so on, and also, having been given some provincial control over immigration, it was seen in some quarters that the thing to do was to bring in as many immigrants from Francophone countries as possible. These immigrants have tended to be from the West Indies. For many Quebeckers, this has posed new group identity problems; the newcomers speak French but they are different in other ways. So there are these extra elements crossing over the boundaries, and changing the equation all the time.

Language in Identity

John Rex: The Quebec nationalist movement has evolved for whatever reasons — historical, partially class-based, socialist, nationalist. The leadership has had to establish markers in the Barthian sense to define that movement. Now for me, one of the interesting things is that it deliberately set out to use language as a marker; a whole batch of language issues were used to mobilise support for the nationalist movement. So you get this rather ridiculous thing about shop signs and a law which stated that immigrant children would have to speak French in the playground.

John Edwards: Yes that's true, but the situation in Quebec has been particular. It has not been difficult to make language a symbol there — and a symbol with content. This is very different from certain other nationalist movements which have had to work much harder in a different way at making language a rallying point for their group. Irish nationalism used the language symbolically but never achieved its goal of actuallly using it. In Quebec, the language was there all the time; it has to be pushed in certain directions, it has to be protected when it comes in contact with English, but it doesn't need to be built from nothing. And it's a very important and potent marker for them.

Dennis Ager: Well, this is the Anglophone/Francophone contrast worldwide. Wherever you are and wherever you happen to have come from in the Francophone world, language is at the centre of the cultural identity. This is not something which is usual or even understandable for an Anglophone. I remember someone commenting that the English wouldn't understand the concept of a language problem in the European Union, because it's not part of the way Anglophones think about these things, whereas the French see that as the prime problem.

John Edwards: Yes, and that does factor in at some level to the lack of ability of Anglophone Canada to understand really what all the fuss is about — this very central and historically strong attachment of language to culture and group.

Sue Wright: No doubt Anglophones would begin to understand if their language looked to be at risk at any time. Could I go back to a point John Rex made earlier about identity being, in part, the 'buzz' you get from speaking the same language? Of course, in situations where the linguistic frontiers are more extensive than the group's, there doesn't have to be congruence. But if we put it the other way around — when the group boundaries are larger than the linguistic boundaries, then there must be a problem. This is precisely the case in the Canadian situation — you do actually have to have communication, there has to be a community of communication for a political entity to work in the democratic participative sense, for there to be any kind of identity at national level. So, although language may not be the strongest marker, in order for the group to work there must be some means of communication, even if this is just a lingua franca.

John Edwards: Yes, but it's a question of which language you're sharing. Are you communicating with the group through what some portion of the group consider your own language, or are you forced, through circumstances, to make this group communication through somebody else's language — or what you are told is somebody else's language?

Sue Wright: And if you are disadvantaged, you have to make a choice at a certain stage, as to whether to make that change and become empowered in the larger group or to refuse assimilation and try to improve the situation of your own group.

John Edwards: Although, of course, sometimes such choices are in fact Hobson's choices.

Charlotte Hoffmann (Salford University): I had been going to ask you the origin of the term 'solitude': you spoke of two solitudes. It seems to sum up this linguistic situation.

John Edwards: A Canadian novelist called Hugh McClelland, wrote a book a few years ago called 'Two Solitudes', referring to French and English-Canada. The title is now being used by everyone in a metaphorical sense with people saying, that's what we are, we'll never come together and so on. But the title actually comes from an earlier poem which talks about two solitudes, which are actually two starting points, coming together and fusing to create a unity out of two things that were separate. So it has quite a different twist in the original sense. But in popular parallels these days it refers to what people imagine to be the situation in Canada.

Charlotte Hoffmann: So there's a slightly resigned, melancholic tinge to it?

John Edwards: Yes, exactly. A feeling that it might have worked out, but we've had so many attempts that it's not going to work out and that we're going to remain in our two solitudes.

Lee Rotherham: In Quebec, the survival of language and of national identity have always been linked. At the turn of the century the nationalists argued that the actual language itself was a protective force for the French-Canadian religion and for French-Canada.

John Edwards: That linking of language and religion makes a lot of sense. To come back to the Irish context, you can find equivalent arguments in De Valera's speeches. There was certainly a popular view that only through Irish could a Catholic Ireland be expressed. In a sense, the stronger marker is being used to support the weaker one.

Helen Kelly-Holmes: Well, independence has negated the language question to a certain extent in Ireland. What is interesting is that language continues to be a factor in Quebec but has all but disappeared as an issue in Ireland. If Quebec obtained independence, would the language be such a major marker of identity, would it even be necessary? Consider the pull factors in the North American environment.

Linda Thompson: Perhaps, once you have independence and establish your own national language, the institutionalisation safeguards the language. This happens even if it has very few mother tongue speakers. Pakistan is a prime example. Speakers of Urdu as a first language made up only 3% of the population when the nation was founded in 1947 and yet it is secure as the national language. Surely French in Quebec is in an even stronger position — it is well-rooted; its speakers are a very large proportion of the population, it has prestige as a language of international communication.

Stephen Barbour: In different parts of the world, at different times, all kinds of different symbols of identity operate, whether this is national identity or ethnic identity or whatever. But even if other markers of identity are often stronger than language — religion, loyalty to the territory, for example — the French language in the Quebec situation appears unassailable because all the cleavages coincide.

The Role of Culture

Lewis Glinert: This issue about how important language is, or what's behind it, raises something which, for me, was very interesting by its absence from your paper. That is the question of the culture and above all literary culture. One perhaps takes for granted in European societies and maybe in others that there is a very firm oral or written literary culture behind the language. What, if any, is the literary culture in Quebec? One takes for granted that in France this is the result of centuries of effort of centralisation and imposition of a certain language, French. Upon this a whole canon of literary culture has been built up and I might have taken for granted that the same would have happened in Quebec. I'm interested to see whether the language question relates to the absence or presence of a literary culture.

Guy Snaith: Well, I'll start by giving a historical perspective. Certainly from the early nineteenth century, there has been a strong Francophone literary tradition. In the early period — before Quebec fell to Wolfe and the British in 1759 — works had been predominantly religious, with a very significant contribution from the Jesuits as well as various other religious orders. Then, after the shock of the fall of Quebec and for most of the eighteenth century there was very little produced. Newspapers, for example, only appeared at the beginning of the nineteenth century.

Lord Durham, in his report of 1839 on the rebellions which had happened two years earlier in Upper and Lower Canada, commented that the French-Canadians were a people with no history and no literature. This was a red rag to the French-Canadian bull. We might date from the Durham Report the production of histories of French-Canada. For example Garneau's *Histoire du Canada* (1845 –1848) set out to inspire French-Canadians, to convince them that they had a heroic history, to congratulate them on surviving for two hundred years in the most adverse of circumstances. Almost immediately, groups appeared whose mission was to encourage the writing of literature in French. A number of the most significant novels which appeared in the nineteenth and in the early twentieth century set out to foster French-Canadian identity, to record the survival of that identity in the face of adversity, to document traditions. The novel, *Les Anciens Canadiens*, which appeared in 1863, was one of the first best-sellers. Such novels demonstrate that this identity was built from a variety of strands: the French language, the Roman Catholic religion, the tradition of large families, commitment to the land and rural life. Themes recur — 'give one daughter and one son to the church and your reward will be in heaven'; 'don't go to Montreal or Quebec City because you will be tarnished, tainted, stained by these bastions of Englishness'. These motifs run through novels like Louis Hémon's *Maria Chapdelaine* which appeared just before the First World War and could still be found in works from the 1930s. So there was a very strong novel tradition which continued into the 1940s and 1950s and which is still going strong today.

Poetry flourished as well. Nelligan, writing at the end of the nineteenth century, was in the Romantic tradition — obviously a bit later than the European movement. This is, however, a feature of Francophone Canada in this period — everything being just about a generation behind.

In the twentieth century, film and *chanson* have had international success. French-Canadian chansonniers and film-makers are well-known outside Quebec — mostly in the Francophone world, but also beyond.

So, I think the French-Canadians do feel there is a very strong literary back-up to their claim of distinctiveness, and in many cases this is more strongly felt than in English-Canada. English-Canada has four times the population of French-Canada, but this is not reflected in literary output. I don't think French-Canadians will feel that English-Canada has produced proportionally more literature or contributed proportionally more to Canadian culture

Peter Noble: As regards the contemporary situation, I would say there's an extraordinarily flourishing literature, which is very rich and diverse. Since the 1950s there's been a tremendous explosion in poetry — for example, Miron, Hébert and Lasnier — and many Quebec critics will tell you that between 1960 and 1980 their best writers were poets, not novelists at all. But that doesn't take away from the fact that the novel-writing tradition has continued and there are many fine novelists working in Quebec today.

Sue Wright: To what extent is there cross-fertilisation with mainstream French culture?

Peter Noble: French-Canadian writers, such as Gabrielle Roy and Antonine Maillet, have won several of the big literary prizes in France and some

French-Canadian writers are now accepted as important members of French literary circles and important contributors to French literary life. This is quite a feat, when one considers that most French-Canadians have a massive inferiority complex about France and there is considerable resentment about the way Quebec is treated in France. For example, in the past, French-Canadian academics couldn't do their doctorate at French universities, although this has changed and now most will have European French rather than Canadian French doctorates. To sum up: yes, there's an extremely flourishing and very important literature into which, I think it's fair to say, the provincial government has poured a great deal of money, providing subsidies for writers and publishers, although this has been cut back recently.

Sue Wright: What about mass culture? Is that equally vibrant?

Guy Snaith: We're now seeing a lot of American-style mini-series and many best-sellers being produced in Quebec.

Peter Noble: And the very important tradition of popular song, the *chanson*, continues.

Sue Wright: And is this mass culture shared with metropolitan France?

Guy Snaith: Yes. Metropolitan France will buy the mini-series but then go on to make snide comments about not being able to understand the language.

Peter Noble: The success and popularity of the French-Canadian *chansonniers* in France is comparable to the situation of the Scots-Gaelic groups in England. They're something a bit different and special, but not to be taken too seriously: they're 'folklore'.

Guy Snaith: But I think there's enough confidence in the literary classes now, for them not to have to go to France to see what's going on there before writing their novels. The pattern now is that, once they have been successful in French-Canada among French-Canadians, then they go to France.

Lee Rotherham: Another interesting development in Canada over the past 25 years has been the courage to speak *Joual* or *Franglais* and to stand up and say, this is an aspect of our life and our language and we have the confidence to portray it to French people.

Guy Snaith: Yes, this confidence did not exist in the past. There was a novel in the 1950s, *La Mort de Mon Joual*, in which the hero goes to France and is very proud because people don't recognise him as French-Canadian because he has polished up his accent. While this was an acceptable notion in the 1950s, by the 1960s, people were no longer doing this; they were writing in the vernacular and saying, this is the way we speak and there are historical reasons for it and there's no need to change our accents.

Peter Noble: We've got to be very careful when we talk about the use of *Joual*, because this variety actually relates to Montreal and there's considerable resentment among French-Canadians that it's used to refer to all of French-Canada, plus the fact that it is regarded by many French-Canadians as decidedly lower-class and therefore they don't want to be identified with it. It may have been at one time a political statement to write in it, but I think most writers have now gone past that and will only use it where it's appropriate. In part their reluctance stems from a recognition that they would restrict their audience in Quebec, let alone outside it.

Sue Wright: So the standard in Francophone Canada is *Grévisse* etc. and writers adhere to the norms of metropolitan France?

Peter Noble: You'll get writers who write absolutely 'pure' French and then you get writers who use lots of anglicisms, lots of calques, lots of syntactical borrowing from US English. Structure and vocabulary have evolved enormously and these borrowings have become ingrained in the French and are now accepted quite happily — at least in North America.

Sue Wright: Does this mean that there is a growing divergence between the written standard and the spoken? What effect does that have? Does it mean that only a member of the elite will read certain books?

Lee Rotherham: There was a major educational reform in the 1950s to reaffirm the standard and stem any slipping towards the Québecois vernacular.

John Edwards: This is a phenomenon you find all over the world. The language people speak in the street is not the variety found in print. By and large, this is not where insuperable problems arise. Difference alone isn't detrimental. What we're seeing now in Quebec is a mature society having the confidence to use these diglossic shifts — it's a great strength. However, where the dialect of a certain group is perceived negatively, that's a different matter.

Sue Wright: But if you see it in terms of a continuum, the further away you get from the norm, the harder it becomes.

John Edwards: But not if people are all taught to read in the same code. This is one of the major arguments for standard English and against producing textbooks in other varieties.

Lewis Glinert: This cultural vitality would lead one to make positive predictions about the future of Quebec's distinctive society and language maintenance in particular.

John Edwards: Yes. But I'm more interested in the question of whether the maintenance of the language and the maintenance of the culture — which we've seen is very vibrant at virtually all levels — is likely to be significantly changed in an independent Quebec. I don't think anybody, nationalist or not, would deny that they have achieved something in terms of culture, historical tradition, founding myths and so on. The question is, how can we best add to that to preserve what we've got? Should we go this route or the other route?

Mike Grover (Multilingual Matters): A further interesting issue about literature is how economics and economic subsidies are used to make political points. For example, when you go to the international book fairs, the French-Canadian bookstand, and the Catalan stand, are bigger than the national stands of Canada and Spain.

Stephen Barbour: What about translations of French-Canadian literature in English-Canada? How popular are they? Because, for example, in Britain translations have an incredibly low level of popularity and I wonder if, despite the tensions between English- and French-speaking Canada, the cultural interchange between those two is possibly much greater than, for example, between Britain and France.

Mike Grover: Yes, it is. And this comes about by the fact that much French-Canadian literature is simply Canadian literature written in French, and so it is also accessible to Anglophone Canadians.

Peter Noble: However, it doesn't go the other way. French-Canadian texts get translated very quickly into English; Anglo-Canadian texts are less popular amongst Francophones.

Guy Snaith: Yes. When one considers someone like Roch Carrier, who has been very successful in translation, the comment was once made by a Quebecker that he writes English in French! So, here we see a kind of inverse snobbery, where Francophones don't want their literature to be too successful in Anglophone Canada.

John Edwards: This might be true, but there's also been a remarkable growth in home-grown Canadian English literature. It's flourishing.

Peter Garrett (University of Wales, Cardiff): We've discussed how some Canadian authors write English in French, which raises the possibility that some of the English speakers are regarded as somewhat French and some parts of the French community are seen as closer to the English community. So, there may in fact be aspects of Frenchness or Englishness which do not have anything to do with geographical location or first language. Is that a possibility in Canada? In Wales, we have found that notions of Englishness and Welshness are quite widely and unevenly distributed among the varieties of Welsh-English. For example, it isn't necessarily along the border areas with England that you find the greatest levels of Englishness, or Welshness associated with varieties spoken in those regions furthest away from the English border: the identities are in fact scattered around in some other way. The divisions aren't simple.

John Rex: But you can still talk of Wales and the Welsh as a 'distinct society', different from England even though there is variation within that society, can't you? I think 'distinct society' is a concept which applies in a very important way to Scotland. There isn't a linguistic basis for mobilising Scottish nationalism but there are many ways in which its institutional differentiation does make it different.

Peter Garrett: I'm not quite sure how far one is justified in seeing Wales as a distinct society. In any event, in our work at Cardiff, we have been looking at how, amongst other things, Welsh identity is mediated through *English* rather than through Welsh, and how regional varieties of English in Wales are differentiated in terms of the degrees of Welshness or Englishness they are perceived to embody and project. Perhaps I can return to the earlier points about the possibility of linguistic markers being superseded by non-linguistic markers where a language disappears and people are left only speaking 'someone else's language'. In the context of Wales, we can see that Welsh identity and cultural continuity are clearly carried through both the Welsh and English languages.

Monolingualism and Bilingualism

Charlotte Hoffmann: In the conclusion to the paper you seem to suggest that there is a move away from institutionalised bilingualism towards greater monolingualism, and in fact today I think the whole debate has been in terms of monolingual or monocultural identities. Do you see societal bilingualism as perhaps disappearing and becoming more a feature of the individual?

John Edwards: Yes. I think that's the way the situation is evolving, despite an official overarching policy of bilingualism. Perhaps there would be last ditch renewed interest and vigour if some separatist scenario were to be played out. But, at the moment, the fact is that, whatever one reads in the reports of the Commissioner of Official Languages, the official language policy has not meant very much in the lives of most Canadians.

Charlotte Hoffmann: But the take-up rate of these immersion courses was a very positive sign, I thought. Do you think that will continue?

John Edwards: Yes, I do. It's rooted in the educational system now.

Charlotte Hoffmann: Even if at the end you don't get bilinguals who use the whole range of their linguistic knowledge would the population still value French immersion courses or heritage language courses? Would they really continue to be a feature of monocultural Canadian society(ies)?

John Edwards: Well, particularly in the case of the latter, the heritage language programmes, I can't see why they would be done away with, especially since in most cases they're not terribly conducive to language retention — they're transitional programmes which aren't meant to have a very long life. I think the popularity of the immersion programmes will decline, but it will take a while for them to tail off. I don't think they are particularly allied to Quebec–Canada relations. So I think there will be an effect, but I don't know exactly when that will occur. But you've touched on an interesting point here: these programmes have processed a few thousand children and what is there to show for that in terms of differences you encounter in normal life? It's disappointing that the products of immersion have not really taken any steps to put what they know into practice, even in those cases where they have the opportunity to do so. But again, this is not a problem which is particular to Quebec, because you have these immersion programmes all over the world and the question is always asked, what happens to the participants?

Peter Noble: Are these programmes seen in terms of bringing economic advantages?

John Edwards: Yes, that's certainly a factor and it's one of the things which could fall away if Canada were to break up. There are other factors too. For example, there was a feeling — which was probably accurate — that children tended to get a better education in immersion classes anyway because they were in smaller groups, because the teachers, by virtue of teaching immersion classes, were likely to be more committed, and because parents who wanted their children to attend such classes were more likely to be people who valued schooling, who would supplement in some way what went on in the classes, and so on. It's a very powerful and positive package which I don't think would just fall away the day after independence.

Sharon Imtiaz: I wanted to ask something with regard to immersion pro-grammes. Are they equally popular both ways? Do you have French children opting for English language immersion programmes?

John Edwards: No, not at all. French children don't need such programmes; it would be submersion for them.

Guy Snaith: With regard to the media, do you think that the Canadian Broadcasting Corporation has played a role in uniting Canada through its television programmes? Or is the CBC seen as the English one and Radio Canada as the French one, again with there being two separate organisations, two more solitudes in Canada — one purveying just English language programmes, the other just French.

John Edwards: Certainly, there is a myth that the CBC links Canada, just like the railway, but to what extent it actually does, I don't know. There's strong reaction when regional programming is sacrificed because of a major production from Toronto. It provides certain obvious links, in that everyone gets their news at the same time, but in terms of the other symbolic freight it's supposed to carry, in helping to define a super-regional Canadian identity, I don't know.

Sharon Imtiaz: Presumably the spread of satellite channels has given access to a number of programmes in different languages.

John Edwards: Yes, of course, the invasion of the satellite channels, particularly from the United States, is having a major effect in Canada — as it is everywhere. In fact satellite is not the main source of US cultural products. CBC itself is regularly hauled over the coals for having too much material from the USA. The latest development here is that the CBC has had to promise to stop buying imports from the USA. Of course, that may well mean that we'll have a lot of programmes from other countries with subtitles. And I'm not being entirely flippant here, because in some quarters the important thing here is not quality, but whether or not a programme comes from the USA.

Monolingualism, Bilingualism, Cultural Pluralism and National Identity: Twenty Years of Language Planning in Contemporary Spain

Charlotte Hoffmann
Department of Modern Languages, University of Salford, Salford M5 4WT, UK

Introduction

Spain, these days, provides a particularly fascinating example of language planning both in terms of policy formulation and in terms of policy implementation. Fascinating are the ambitions underlying many of the language policies, the speed with which they have been formulated and set in motion, the extent to which they have begun to affect many spheres of public life in many parts of the Iberian Peninsula, and fascinating, too, are the results which are beginning to become apparent. It is also a process which is, for many Spaniards, controversial. For linguists, both inside and outside Spain, the public debate on linguistic issues which Spanish language planning has sparked off is both dramatic and illuminating.

It seems that the Iberian Peninsula has always been multilingual as a result of different tribes and peoples settling there. After the Roman invasion and occupation of Iberia a Romance language continuum emerged that yielded many different varieties whose status, use and development changed over the centuries according to political circumstances. The development of the variety known as Castilian is closely connected with the history of the development of a Spanish centralised state which, in turn, is closely tied up with the dominance of monolingualism. It has always been the case that the non-Castilian languages suffered and Spain's regions on the periphery became weaker in the same measure as the centre became stronger and Castilian asserted its supremacy over the other languages of Spain.

The development of this supremacy of Castilian is an important theme in Spanish history. And the way in which Spain's history has been presented to the outside world — and during most of her past to her own population as well — has seldom gone beyond trying to create the image of a united monolingual nation state with emphasis placed on a strong Spanish national identity. Regional languages and different cultural customs were acknowledged to be part of Spain's national heritage although generally not given much prominence. As has been the case in other, somewhat artificially created, nation states, the central government has tended to be at variance with the phenomenon of separate regional identities which in many cases are inseparably tied to the regional language. The co-existence of national and regional identities does not necessarily create problems, but for the central government it has, more often than not,

1352 0520/95/01 0059-32 $10.00/0

represented a delicate balancing act which has tended to end in conflict whenever Spaniards had a particular identity (usually the national patriotic one) hoisted upon them.

Thus, not surprisingly, regional loyalties and identities are also central themes in Spanish history. They may be linked to a particular regional language and that seems to be the case certainly with the three most important ones (important in terms of status, use and number of users): Catalan, Galician and Basque. John Hooper suggests that Spaniards, more that most Europeans elsewhere, tend to put their regional loyalties on a par with, or even ahead of, loyalty to the state and that such sentiments have bedevilled attempts to build a strong unified state throughout Spanish history. In fact, in order of importance, loyalty to one's native town or village, the *patria chica*, precedes loyalty to the region. Such sentiments, and a number of other factors — historical, cultural and geographical — 'have combined to divide Spaniards from each other and to produce in any of them the conviction that the region comes first and the state comes second and, in extreme cases, nowhere at all' (Hooper, 1995: 372).

Regional languages were barely tolerated during much of Franco's long rule — and indeed for much of the time in this and previous centuries as well. They could not be used as official languages in their areas, nor were they used in education, at the workplace, or in the media. They did not receive any kind of state support, so that by the end of the Franco era not only had the number of speakers been decimated, but also the number of functions for which regional languages were used had become reduced and popular attitudes towards them had become manipulated. The literature is full of accounts of the ruthless and systematic suppression of the native languages of Catalonia, Galicia, and the Basque Country where it was especially fierce because of the fear of Basque separatism.

Taking a more global view, it should, however, be noted that Castilian assumed its pre-eminent role not solely by dint of repression and coercion. Language change is a social process which is driven along by the linguistic behaviour of speakers. It is true that, in part, such behaviour may be influenced by punitive measures on the part of the state. But it is equally true that some languages become more successful candidates for language spread. Over the centuries Castilian Spanish has been an efficient means of communication adopted by many, on its merits rather than by force.

Apart from effectively reducing the status and use of regional languages in Franco's Spain, the suppression of them also had a very different effect: they fuelled many people's determination to fight for their survival. More often than not the Catalan, Galician and Basque languages became symbols of resistance to the authoritarian, centralist policies of the Madrid government. John Green (1993: 156–7) says:

> That Catalan, Basque and Galician should be the three minority languages most often mentioned is in no way surprising, since they were the three most ruthlessly suppressed by the Franco regime in the years following the Civil War, and the first to benefit from the more liberal climate in the 1970s. It is a moot point whether their present vigour is partly owed to the severity of their repression and to the resistance it engendered: in Catalonia at least,

the attempt to relegate Catalan to the status of a rural patois was perceived not only as a social injustice but also as an insult to a proud cultural heritage.

It is therefore not surprising that when democracy was established, the fight against language shift became a priority for the new Autonomous Communities (or self-governing regions), and this was coupled with the assertion that Spain's newly-proclaimed policy of pluralism concerned language as an expression of regional identity. According to its new democratic constitution Spain has 17 *Comunidades Autónomas*; in the following I will deal with the three that are generally agreed to have both a historical claim to a separate identity and their own language (they are referred to as the *comunidades históricas*): Catalonia, Galicia and the Basque Country.

In view of their history, the recent preoccupation with matters concerning language contact, linguistic conflict, language recovery and bilingual education in the three above-mentioned regions is not surprising. In Catalonia, and to a lesser extent in Galicia and the Basque Country, a growing interest in sociolinguistic concerns began to emerge in the 1960s and was continued in the 1970s, that is, in the years of Spain's transition to democracy; this interest went beyond the more traditional literary and philological studies of these languages that there had been before.

Language planning took off in the 1970s. It involves a large number of variables — historical, political, economic, social, cultural and linguistic — as well as several languages and linguistic varieties whose linguistic status is less well-defined. It is estimated that today approximately a quarter of all Spaniards speak a regional language in addition to, or instead of, the official language of the state, Castilian Spanish. In the three areas to be examined here, language planning is being carried out within a clearly defined legal framework and put in place by committed regional governments which support language policies in many different ways.

That the motives behind such support are not always sustained by a sound sociolinguistic evaluation of a region's linguistic and social situation should come as no surprise. But some 15 years after the Autonomies' language policies were first formulated there is still widespread popular support for language recovery and many of the measures that have been taken to ensure it. However, there are also those who feel uneasy with some of the more radical aspects of language policies and the wider effects they are having on the lives of those who are affected by them — the bilingual speakers of regional languages and the monolingual Castilian speakers.

Naturally, language planning cannot be considered in isolation. It is closely bound up with the general socioeconomic and cultural development of a region, and ultimately it derives its impetus from political decisions. Spain's experiment with a quasi-federal, pluricultural democracy has not been an easy one. It has been fraught with the difficulties encountered in the attempts to solve the problems raised by Basque separatism and ETA terrorism, and also (and more relevantly for my discussion here), a worry about the dangers inherent in the perceived potential rise in Catalan nationalist aspirations on the one hand and, on the other, the possibility of a centralist military backlash.

The situation in which the regional languages have found themselves has been a reflection of the more general political problems affecting the country as a whole. In the days of the old Franco regime, opposition to the clampdown on Catalan, Galician and Basque was a strong unifying force. Now the suppression has disappeared and with it, its unifying effect. Some argue that the threat to non-Castilian languages has not yet been removed: 'The freedom that the present rather fragile democracy has brought could turn out to be even more harmful to the minority languages of Spain than oppressive dictatorship' (Wardhaugh, 1987: 120). The perceived threat to the minority languages is still used to emphasise the need to promote regional language policies designed as part of the overall political strategies of the autonomous governments. I agree that a threat still exists. But it is of an entirely different kind from what it was in the past and it affects a new set of people in an unprecedented kind of way.

My aim in this contribution is to look at the goals of language planning in the three Autonomous Communities of Catalonia, the Basque Country and Galicia, and to examine the results which the application of a particular model have brought about. The central issues pertaining to language planning, language promotion and bilingualism will be discussed within the context of issues relating to monolingualism, cultural pluralism and identity.

As will be seen, there have been significant successes: Catalan is fast becoming the language of the Principality of Catalonia, and in *Euskadi* the decline of the Basque language seems to have been arrested. But in their pursuit of 'linguistic normalisation' (which is the term for language recovery used in the Spanish contexts), language planners may risk becoming guilty of the same kind of excesses as were committed by centralist language planners of the past who were concerned with ensuring the hegemony of Castilian Spanish to the detriment of the other linguistic varieties. In other words, in some respects language planners appear to be starting to repeat the very same injustices they originally set out to redress: the results of the attempts to change the linguistic behaviour of certain communities seem to be, to some extent, counterproductive, for reasons that I shall examine.

It is my contention that language planners in at least two of the three areas under discussion will need to reassess their policies and lower their objectives so as to ensure the continued support of majority public opinion and to prevent the issue from becoming one that divides and harms their societies. This may involve embracing a more permanent state of societal bilingualism in Catalonia and a slower pace of promotion of the Galician language in Galicia.

Background

General sociopolitical issues

The approval of Spain's new democratic constitution in 1978 marks the formal transition of the country from a highly centralised state to a quasi-federal one characterised by cultural and linguistic pluralism. The extent to which the 17 Autonomous Regions that make up the Spanish state enjoy their own powers of decision compares very favourably in many respects with the degree of self-government found among the countries following the fully federal model.

Decentralisation has made it possible for regional diversity to be developed and institutionalised through legislation passed by the autonomous governments.

The three *comunidades históricas* have gone furthest in language planning. They have a historical claim to autonomy, that is, a clearly distinct cultural identity which includes the possession of a linguistic variety generally accepted as a language in its own right. They certainly have, although to varying degrees, all the linguistic as well as sociolinguistic features considered important for such a claim to be upheld (see, for instance, Bell's 1976 discussion of formal and functional typologies based on three different models). Other regions have also given special status to their regional varieties in their Statutes of Autonomy so that, for instance, *Vascuence* (a name for a particular Basque variety) is recognised as Navarre's special language and *Valencià (Valencian)* as that of Valencia. And certain other Autonomous Communities, such as Aragón, Asturias and the Canary Islands, include in their Statutes the commitment to promote their particular variety of Castilian.

Notice, incidentally, that when Spain adopted in 1978 the model of a democratic state which Spaniards called *el estado de las autonomías* (i.e. a decentralised model based on regional self-government), the justification for this model was that *some* of the Autonomous Regions undoubtedly had a historical claim to their own separate identity. There were only three of them to start with: Catalonia, the Basque Country and Galicia. The most distinctive mark on which these claims were founded was the existence of their own language in the respective territories. It was then felt that the other regions also could have a claim to autonomy, but a less convincing one than the *comunidades históricas*. This feeling was written into the 1978 Spanish Constitution by allowing for two different degrees of autonomy, which we can call full autonomy and partial autonomy. This is an important fact that was to become very influential later in the minds of Spaniards. It is also significant that the Statutes of Autonomy were approved in a chronological order that reflected the strength of the respective claims in a way which paralleled the convictions of the Spanish people regarding the status of their languages: Catalonia's Statute was passed first, in 1979, followed by the Basque Statute in the same year and shortly afterwards Galicia's in 1980. There was public debate on the linguistic and other merits of the claim of Andalusia to either full or less than full autonomic status, and eventually this region (which does not have its own language but is nevertheless both linguistically and culturally clearly different from Castile and the rest of Spain) achieved full autonomy in 1981.

Cultural and linguistic questions

The preceding 40 years of Franco's dictatorship (1936–1975) had seen the promotion of one national language, Castilian Spanish, and one national identity, *una sola Hispanidad*. Whereas pride in and identification with the *patria chica*, one's regional/local place of origin and/or residence, was considered part of every Spaniard's personality and could be glorified in folkloristic ways, all other forms of ethnic or national otherness expressed in different languages were looked upon as politically suspect. Not surprisingly, the other languages of Spain became associated with political dissent and were thus suppressed. It must not be forgotten that during Spain's long post-Civil War period, which was characterised by acute economic poverty and cultural underdevelopment (it was called *'un páramo cultural'* or 'cultural wilderness', in a famous phrase used by José Luis Abellán, a well-known Spanish writer), the various regional varieties, Basque, Galician and, to a lesser degree, Catalan were often seen as the languages of the uneducated rural populations. The implied stance was that monolingualism in Castilian was some kind of virtue that everyone should aspire to and enable their children to achieve.

To the foreign sociolinguist it may seem odd, but to the Spaniard it is apparently not at all surprising that there have never been clear answers to questions such as how many linguistic varieties exist in Spain, which of these are languages in their own right, and how many speakers each of them have or have had. At any rate, in the past, such answers as were given appear to have been based on political expediency and cultural bias. A handbook written by the Jesuit Father Ignacio Menéndez Reigada called *Catecismo patriótico español*, published in Salamanca in 1939, has this to say on the question of whether any other languages besides Castilian are spoken in Spain:

> It may be said that in Spain only the Castilian language is spoken, for apart from it, only Basque is spoken, which is used as the only language in a few hamlets alone; it is reduced to the functions of a dialect because of its linguistic and philological poverty.

In answer to the question of what the main dialects spoken in Spain are, he suggests four: Catalan, Valencian, Majorcan and Galician (quoted in Comet i Codia 1990; the translation is not mine). This may serve as an example reflecting the prevailing climate just at the end of Spain's Civil War.

More recently, a highly respected linguist, dialectologist and member of the Spanish Royal Academy, Gregorio Salvador (1987), wrote that he recognised ten other languages besides Castilian. He lists Galician, Aranese (which he specifies as a dialect of Gascon), Catalan and then three varieties of Basque and four of Navarrese (the name given to the varieties of Basque spoken in Navarre). He considers the varieties of the last two groups to be separate languages on the basis of their clear linguistic differentiation from each other, which result in problems of intercommunication, and their close link to a particular geographical territory. He is obviously using mainly linguistic criteria. He does not consider Valencian to be a separate language, but rather a dialect of Catalan. Elsewhere in his book he makes the clear distinction between the four languages with official status (Castilian, Basque, Catalan and Galician) and other linguistic varieties, some of which he refers to as *otras lenguas imaginadas o proclamadas* ('other imagined or so-called languages' Salvador, 1987: 100). He attacks here those people in other autonomous regions who — in his opinion, misguidedly — advocate a higher status for their linguistic variety than can be justified on linguistic or historical grounds.

The official view of the Spanish government, as expressed in its publication *'España 94'*, a kind of yearbook designed to provide facts and background information, is that 'the Constitution recognises the right of the Autonomous Communities of the Basque Country, Galicia, Catalonia, the Balearic Islands and the Community of Valencia to use their own languages without jeopardising the use of Castilian Spanish' — which, although not quite accurate (see below), does indicate which are considered to be the official languages of Spain (they are named in the next sentence as *el euskera, el gallego, el catalán y el valenciano*). About Valencian, it says that 'it is considered, by the majority of linguists, to be a variety of Catalan'. The Catalan-speaking area, according to '*España 94*', includes both the Balearic Islands, parts of Aragón and Murcia, the Principality of Andorra, the French Rousillon and the Italian city of Algher (Sardinia). Notice, by the way, that this book also mentions that Gascon is spoken in the Valle de Arán (Catalan Pyrenees) and Portuguese in a few frontier areas in Castilla-León and Extremadura. No other living language is named (except some of the ones spoken by foreign residents in Spain).

Writing about multilingualism in Spain, Miquel Siguán, a Catalan sociolinguist, deals separately with the four languages of Spain which enjoy official status (Castilian, Basque, Galician and Catalan, including Valencian, he says) and then seems to suggest a somewhat different category of 'other languages and linguistic varieties'. Asturian (or *Bable*), Aranese and Aragonese are discussed under that heading (Siguán, 1992). Incidentally, very few authors mention the existence of some 16,000 Portuguese speakers in Spain (see previous paragraph) — not a big number, to be sure, but nevertheless a linguistic minority that seems to be ignored by many.

One might have expected Spain's 1978 Constitution to bring clarity into the question of the number of languages, but it does not. It mentions 'the other languages of Spain' that are to be official in their respective autonomous regions, and it refers to 'distinctive linguistic varieties' without, however, spelling out which these might be. In the constitutions of other officially bilingual or multilingual states the official languages are mentioned by name (e.g. in those of Switzerland and Finland). The Final Provision of the Spanish Constitution stipulates that it is to be published 'in the other Spanish languages'. The Constitution was, in fact, published in Castilian, Basque, Catalan, Galician and Valencian (the Catalan and Valencian texts that I have seen differ minimally). It is unclear whether one should interpret this as an implied recognition, in the constitutional text, of five different languages. On the other hand, in 1978 people did not know which regions were going to seek statutes of full autonomy, or which exactly would consider that they had a distinct 'own language' (some might have guessed that Catalonia and the Basque Country would make both territorial and linguistic claims, but the future was much more uncertain in the case of, say, the Valencia region), so perhaps it was wise for the Constitution to be cautious on language questions.

In view of Spain's long-standing neglect of its linguistic minorities, it comes as little surprise that for many years there were no exact figures on the number of speakers of languages other than Castilian Spanish. As has been (and still is) the case in other European states, national censuses in the past did not include a language question. Today, more reliable figures are beginning to emerge, as many of the Spanish autonomous regions are compiling statistics on the use and knowledge of the languages spoken in their communities. Even so, it will be some time before a full picture emerges, as administrative boundaries do not coincide with linguistic ones. Thus, for example, Galician is spoken in parts of Asturias and in some provinces of León and Zamora, and Catalan can be found in the Aragonese provinces of Huesca, Zaragoza and Teruel. In these places minority language speakers are not given any linguistic protection, nor do they count in the statistics.

This is one of the weaknesses of the territoriality principle upon which Spain's pluralism is founded. What is more, on the whole it is becoming more and more difficult to apply this principle at all in trying to arrive at a theoretical explanation of Spain's multilingualism today, because large-scale immigration has diluted the original linguistic cohesion of many of Spain's regions.

An assessment of Spain's language planning must take into account Spain's traditional distrust of bilingualism, whether it is considered on a societal or an individual level. This suspicion is in line with a long European tradition which links language and politics within the context of the Nation State (see, for instance, Hoffmann, 1991: 203–4). Bilingualism was seen as a historical accident which could easily lead to weak government and thus was something to be avoided. The basic assumption was, and all too often still is, that bilingualism leads to conflict resulting from the fight for dominance of a particular language, culture or geographical space. Such conflict can only be avoided by either marginalising minorities or by pursuing policies which aim to reach consensus. Before cultural pluralism became part of the political agenda, this consensus, had, in most cases been interpreted as meaning assimilation. Prolonged pressure on minorities to assimilate, or to accept their marginalised position in the interests of the nation, had enabled many European states to develop in such a way that political boundaries were perceived as coinciding with national and cultural (including linguistic) ones. Minorities have tended to be contained in certain territories, often found at the periphery of the state, and many have lived in continuous conflict of interest with the centre that sought to control their political, economic and cultural life. (Among Spanish writers, see, for example, Tovar, 1982 or Paniagua Fuentes, 1991.)

From a sociolinguistic point of view, this has led to what some describe as *conflict diglossia*. The meaning of the term 'diglossia', in the Spanish literature, tends to go beyond the framework of the classic interpretation proposed by Ferguson or Fishman. In the Spanish context the term is used to describe language contact between Castilian and a non-Castilian language where the language of the dominant centre is imposed by the state on another language. This implies not only that speakers of non-Castilian languages have seen a curtailment of their linguistic rights to use their own language for the functions of their choice, or at least certain well-defined functions, but also that the dominant language has had an impoverishing effect on the regional languages themselves. In particular, Catalan and Galician sociolinguists have written about Castilian as the *dominant language* and of Catalan as the language that had become *minorised* (Strubell i Trueta, 1993: 187).

Social and economic factors

This century has, in a very real way, seen powerful economic and social forces, of the kind usually associated with language shift, at work in each of the three

Spanish regions referred to above. Migration, industrialisation, urbanisation, conscription into military service (organised on a national basis), wider access to education and the media have all contributed towards rapid castilianisation. Towards the end of the Franco era, repression of the regional languages became somewhat less severe, and a modest amount of public use of Basque and Catalan could be observed. But a massive shift away from Catalan and Basque had been set in motion as a result of the languages not having been used for a variety of functions or in the media, and also because of negative public attitudes towards them. Castilian Spanish had become the language associated with social progress and therefore parents were keen to enable their children to become fluent users of it, thereby accepting it into their homes even if previously the regional language had been the language of the family.

In Galicia the sociolinguistic situation was rather different. Galician continued to be used as an oral form of communication among the rural population but became heavily stigmatised, and Castilian was generally required as the language for social advancement; it had always been the language of written communication. Galician was, therefore, very much in a diglossic relationship with Castilian. Language has never been the same kind of issue in Galicia as in the other two regions. This fact caused Wardhaugh to refer to the Galicians as 'one of the more dormant linguistic minorities in Europe today' (1987: 127).

The three regions share some features, such as their geographical situation on the fringe of the country, their history of suppression and neglect, their desire to maintain their cultural distinctiveness, their fear of language loss and linguistic inadequacy and a consequent commitment to language promotion. All three perceive themselves as ethnically different from other Spaniards; and their languages, for them, represent the expression of their ethnic, if not national, identity. But otherwise there are more differences than similarities. Whereas Catalonia and the Basque Country have long been two of Spain's most powerful economic areas, Galicia has a long history of being one of the poorest. Catalonia and the Basque country have attracted vast numbers of migrants from other parts of Spain, while Galicia saw millions of her people migrate to other parts of Spain or abroad.

With regard to demographic considerations, too, there are marked differences. Most of Galicia's almost three million inhabitants are of Galician decent and while Galician is said to be understood by most of them, over three-quarters (80%) are said to be able to speak it. In Catalonia, likewise, a very large number of the population are said to understand Catalan (90%) and over two-thirds of Catalonia's six and a half million inhabitants are able to use Catalan, both in its written and its oral form. However, Catalonia has experienced immigration on such a massive scale that today only about half its population is of Catalan descent and it is feared, in some circles, that by the year 2040 there will be no 'pure' Catalans left at all (Hooper, 1995).

In terms of the sociolinguistic distribution of its speakers, only Catalan can be said to have been supported consistently by an articulate middle class which conferred positive values on the language, ensured a certain amount of familiarity with literacy in Catalan, even at times of suppression, and then provided Catalan society with speakers able to occupy influential positions in the new Autonomous community. The very large immigrant element in Catalan society (which in some cities, including Barcelona, makes up for more than half of the local population) constitutes a sizeable minority which is beginning to resist some of the language policies designed to make all Catalonia Catalan-speaking. More about this later.

In the Basque Country there is also a large immigrant element. Some 30% of inhabitants are assumed to be of non-Basque origin but most of them are not recent immigrants. Basque is very much the language of a minority of Euskadi's 2.2 million inhabitants. It is understood by less than half and spoken, at the most, by a quarter of the population (probably much less). Like Galician, and unlike Catalan, it cannot look back on a long literary tradition, nor has Basque drawn its speakers mainly from the middle classes and the region's intelligentsia. Whereas Catalan aspirations have tended towards greater independence from Madrid, the political agenda of many prominent Basques has often veered towards separatism.

To sum up, one can say that in Spain, linguistic diversity has succeeded in continuing to exist against a backdrop of enforced institutionalised monolingualism (which was reflected in the term chosen for the dominant language: Spanish, i.e. the language of *all* Spaniards). Today, approximately 25% of the population have a non-Castilian first language and about 40% of Spain's inhabitants live in an official bilingual area (Willis, 1992). Although the actual bilingual territory constitutes only 18% of Spain, the country is clearly multilingual.

Normally one would expect to come across terms such as 'minority language' and 'linguistic minority' in the context of language planning in a multilingual state. This terminology is not, however, used in the Spanish literature on the subject, perhaps because it can be interpreted in different ways: *vis-à-vis* the monolingual Castilians in Spain as a whole, speakers of Galician or Catalan are a minority, but in the territory where their language is spoken, they are not. Therefore, expressions such as 'the language of the Autonomous Community' or 'the languages of Spain' prevail. In relation to language recovery the above-mentioned term 'minorised language' usefully indicates the status of a linguistic variety and suggests that only by rejecting its subordinate status will the language in question ultimately be able to demonstrate that it can fight on equal terms in the competition for users, and thus survive.

Language Planning in Spain after 1978

The background against which the new democratic Constitution and subsequent related legislation had to be worked out was Spain's long history of friction between the centre and the periphery. A quasi-federal system would enable the regions, several of them concerned about their own language, to address the conflicts of the past by assuming responsibility for their own cultural and linguistic affairs. For the centre, the acceptance of cultural pluralism and linguistic diversity was probably seen, in part, as a means of ensuring the preservation of other central powers for the state.

The upshot was that the linguistic model that was decided upon follows the territoriality principle and therefore devolves to the regions the power to determine their own linguistic policies. Apart from two short periods in Spain's history, this is the first time that her minority languages have enjoyed legal rights. By not opting for the personality principle, which gives rights to the speakers of minority languages independently of where they reside, the Spanish state has no doubt avoided conflict with the regions. But by the same token a different set of problems has been created: speakers of, say, Catalan or Basque outside Catalonia or *Euskadi* cannot claim any linguistic rights, and the immigrants in Catalonia or Galicia do feel, on occasions, that their linguistic rights are being violated by the autonomous language policies, which are aimed primarily at the protection and promotion of Catalan and Galician respectively.

The driving forces behind language planning in Spain were twofold: on the political side there was the desire for political and cultural self-determination. Independence from Madrid would be easier to achieve if the language of the Autonomous Community became the official one in that region. This objective was supported by the generally accepted view that there exists a very close link between language and national identity which should be expressed through self-government. This idea was upheld by many writers on the subject, politicians as well as linguists, and it was incorporated in the pertinent legislation which developed the respective Statutes of Autonomy; it was also used quite prominently in linguistic campaigns. However, the notion of linking language with national identity is not without its problems, as it begs the question of who or what decides the identity that people in a given area are supposed to have.

The other strong reason for language planning was to ensure the survival of the languages, a concern shared by many who otherwise were less interested in politics. Not only had Catalan, Basque and Galician given way to Castilian Spanish in many public and private domains, so that transmission from one generation to the next was no longer assured, but the languages themselves had become castilianised in various ways — through extensive lexical borrowing and grammatical interference, for instance.

The legal basis for language planning in Spain has been articulated in three different types of legislation: the 1978 Constitution, the Statutes of Autonomy of the individual Communities and their Linguistic Normalisation Laws. I shall deal with the former here and the latter two in the next section.

The Preamble to the Constitution asserts the protection of all Spaniards 'in the exercise of their human rights, their cultures and traditions, languages and institutions' (my translation). Spain's multilingualism is recognised explicitly in Articles 3, 20, 148 and in its Final Provision. The provisions set out are of a general nature and several commentators have remarked on the fact that, at times, the wording of the Constitution is vague or ambivalent. This vagueness is commonly seen as deliberate, and as an inevitable consequence of consensus politics. In this respect, Mar-Molinero and Stevenson (1991: 167) refer to the 'spirit of compromise which pervades each clause'. The cornerstone of Spanish linguistic policies is Article 3:

(1) Castilian is the official Spanish language of the state. All Spaniards have a duty to know it and the right to use it.
(2) The other languages of Spain shall also have official status in their respective Autonomous Communities, in accordance with their Statutes.

(3) The wealth of the various linguistic varieties in Spain is a cultural heritage which shall be the object of special respect and protection. (My translation.)

Note that Mar-Molinero uses the following translation:

(3) The richness of Spain's linguistic variety is a cultural heritage which shall be the object (etc.)

Cobarrubias and Garmendia Lasa (1987) choose a more literal rendering of the Spanish (which is: (3) *La riqueza de las distintas modalidades lingüísticas de España es un patrimonio cultural que será objeto de especial respeto y protección*):

(3) The wealth of the different linguistic modalities in Spain is a cultural patrimony (etc.)

This is an often-quoted clause, partly because of the nature of the provisions enshrined in it, and partly because it illustrates the Constitution's ambiguities. As far as constitutions go, Clause 1 is quite unique in the way it specifies both the citizens' rights and their duties *vis-à-vis* Castilian Spanish, and it establishes its supremacy. Clause 2 recognises the other languages of Spain, which may also be official, without, however, spelling out which languages they are; it also assigns the responsibility for language planning to the Autonomous Communities. In Mar-Molinero's interpretation this clause also restricts the concept of plurilingualism to two languages only in each Community, and to discrete geographical areas.

Clause 3 is the most ambiguous one. It uses quite open-ended wording and concepts. It also reflects the linguistic uncertainty alluded to earlier — a comparison of the three translations demonstrates this. To the sociolinguist, 'linguistic modalities' is too general a concept; and neither 'linguistic modalities' nor 'linguistic varieties' specify which languages or dialects are referred to. Nor does the clause spell out who is responsible for protecting these linguistic varieties against those who refuse to recognise, let alone protect them.

In Article 20, the Constitution states that the law shall guarantee to 'significant social and political groups' the access to 'the means of social communication controlled by the state or any other public body, within a framework of respect for the pluralism of society and the various languages of Spain' (my translation). What is not spelt out, however, is which 'social groups' these are. Whoever they may be, however, it is a fact that very little use of regional languages is made by the state-controlled media.

According to Article 148 (Clause 17) the Autonomous Communities assume responsibility for the promotion of culture, research and, where applicable, the teaching of the regional languages. The Statutes of Autonomy of the individual communities give further details about how this responsibility should be carried out.

In cases of conflict between national and regional legislation, the Constitutional Tribunal is called upon to adjudicate. This has happened on a number of occasions already, in cases of major legislative importance such as deciding on the constitutionality of a Law of Linguistic Normalisation, as well as in cases of a more personal nature, such as the issue of whether a Catalan politician has the right to address the *Cortes* (or national parliament) in Catalan, or whether it is constitutional that a knowledge of the regional language should be required as part of the professional competence that a person must have to qualify for an official administrative position in a particular autonomous community.

Formulating language policies was, of course, primarily a matter for the politicians. But there has been a very strong input from linguists and sociolinguists, first and foremost Catalan ones, many of whom have looked carefully at language planning, particularly with regard to bilingual education, carried out in other parts of the world, notably Wales and Canada. The dissemination of ideas and information has been very helpful to many an interested outsider, even though invariably it has been, ideologically, a somewhat one-sided process.

The aim of all linguistic policies has been the promotion of regional languages by declaring them the official language of the autonomous region, together with Castilian Spanish. In effect, this has meant a general recognition of widespread societal and individual bilingualism. In Catalonia, however, language planners are willing to accept equal status for the two languages only as a transitional position, but their real aim is to achieve a situation in which a mainly Catalan-speaking Catalonia will use its own language for most public functions and keep the use of Spanish to the minimum necessary.

It is clear, then, that language planning in Spain embraces both status and corpus planning. As regards status planning, many of the measures taken have been designed to promote the use of the regional languages in most spheres of public life, with special emphasis given to education. As far as corpus planning is concerned, the policies followed have led to the setting up of bodies entrusted with the codification and elaboration of the languages so as to equip them adequately for their use as official languages.

The Spanish Language Planning Model

As we have seen, Spanish linguistic terminology can be quite different from that used by sociolinguists writing in English. The term, or rather programmatic title, under which language planning policies have been designed and carried out in all three regions is *linguistic normalisation*. The first formal discussion of the nature of normalisation appears in a book by Ninyoles: 'Normalisation entails placing a language on an equal footing with other languages (neither higher nor lower: at the same level')' (1972: 75). This is obviously an aspect of status planning. In the same discussion Ninyoles also expresses the opinion that normalisation presupposes standardisation, and that language planning is the method through which it can be achieved.

The official definition of the term *normalisation* which many Catalans writing on the subject seem to have adopted goes back to a Resolution formulated at the end of the Congress of Catalan Culture which was held in 1975–1977. Torres (1984: 59–60) renders it into English in the following way: '[it is] a process during which a language gradually recovers the formal functions it had lost and at the same time works its way into those social sectors, within its own territory, where it was not spoken before.' What is on the agenda here, then, is *language spread* as well as *language recovery*, as the process involves the extension of language functions into new areas, with the intention of reversing the previous diglossic situation.

Normalisation is seen by all the three peoples, but more emphatically in the case of the Catalans, as a means of providing a link with the past, the time when the currency of each language was real (as well as official in Catalonia) in its local area, in the Middle Ages and, more recently, during brief but significant periods earlier this century. Thus, an often repeated claim is that there is historical justification for restoring these languages to their rightful places. It was widely felt, in all cases, that the efforts, carried out during the latter part of the life of the Second Spanish Republic in the 1930s to re-establish the regional languages had been interrupted illegitimately (by Franco's rising against the democratic Republic, which provoked the 1936–1939 Civil War), and that these efforts should be resumed with the same objectives.

The Basques and Galicians modelled their policies, including the legal framework within which they were set, closely on the Catalan scheme. In all three regions the use of the term *normalisation* encompasses the two important, interlinking aspects of planning, language development and elaboration of function (as part of status planning) which are included under the concept of 'norm', namely: (1) the codification of the language, i.e. formulation of linguistic norms; and (2) the social extension of these norms for wider, everyday use. In other words, the promotion of regional languages consists of two parallel activities: providing the necessary linguistic tools, and planning for the normal use of Catalan, Basque and Galician in all functional domains. The thinking behind this is that, as a consequence of this two-pronged process, the status of the languages will be enhanced — and, in that sense, the resulting situation will be more 'normal'.

However, given that the socioeconomic and demographic conditions today are quite different from what they were in the 1930s, the promotion of regional languages is likely to seem less attractive if it is carried out under the banner of restoration of a situation that existed in the past, since the composition of present-day Catalan, Basque and Galician society, as well as the depth and richness of contemporary cultural life there, are very different from what they were 60 years ago.

The Statutes of Autonomy, passed by each regional parliament, lay down the status of the languages to be used in their area and guarantee to the citizens of the Communities the right to use them. Accordingly, Catalan, Basque and Galician have become in law the respective Autonomies' 'own language', a fact which allows them to be promoted above all other languages, as they are awarded co-official status with Castilian. The concept of *lengua propia* ('own language'), which appears in all three Statutes, has been picked out by some (non-Spanish) commentators. In English it sounds somewhat idiosyncratic, as it is neither a recognised linguistic term nor a legal one. However, it lends itself to be associated with two important issues: seeing language as part of the cultural heritage and a symbol of identity; and appearing as a vehicle of social integration, justifying in this way its status as an official language.

Within a short space of time, between November 1982 and June 1983, Laws of Linguistic Normalisation were passed in all three Autonomous Communities, detailing the aims and provisions of the governments' language policies. Again, the similarity between the three Laws is quite striking. They all establish co-official status between their own language and Castilian Spanish, confirm their citizens' rights to know and use both languages, and declare that any form of linguistic discrimination is illegal. These Laws aim to promote the region's own language in all aspects of community life (including local and regional administration, the legal system, the media and education), and they set out the means by which these objectives are going to be realised.

If we compare the Laws with one another we find that there is varying emphasis concerning certain linguistic issues, and that the institutions within each region made responsible for the implementation of the Statutes and for advising on linguistic matters are also somewhat different. Other differences in the Normalisation Laws point towards the specific cultural and linguistic traditions of each Autonomous Community. This is particularly noticeable in their Preambles. In the Catalan one, three lengthy clauses explain the specific significance Catalan has for the Catalan people in terms of identity and as an integrative tool for communication, and they deal with the precarious situation in which the language finds itself after years of official disuse. The Galician Preamble is shorter but uses much stronger language. It mentions the 'profoundly negative' consequences that two centuries of centralist government have had for Galicia, and it refers to the 'political depersonalisation and cultural marginalisation' that has 'increasingly impoverished the Galician people' (my translations). Here, too, the link between language and identity is enshrined in the text, and the widespread use of the Galician language is seen as a way of uniting Galicians within Galicia and, interestingly, also beyond its boundaries.

The Basque Law has a slightly different title: *Ley de normalización del uso del euskera* (1986), which according to Mar-Molinero the Basques themselves translated into English as 'The Basic Law of the Standardisation of the Use of Basque'. Mar-Molinero considers this significant: 'For the Basques it is the "use" that is to be normalised, for the Catalans the language itself' (1990: 56). The authorised English translations of the other two Autonomies' Laws use 'linguistic normalisation'. The Basque choice of the term 'standardisation' is interesting, too, as it expresses just one specific aspect of normalisation. Perhaps this is due to the fact that standardisation was a particularly thorny issue in the case of this language (one must bear in mind that some linguists, like Salvador, 1987, claim, as was mentioned earlier, that there are no fewer than *seven* mutually unintelligible Basque languages). Like the other two Laws, the Basque one stresses the link between language and identity in the Preamble, which states that 'Basque is to be recognised as the most visible and objective marker of identity of our Community'. Although these Laws were passed by the respective legislative bodies at the beginning of the 1980s, they had to wait until June 1986 to be finally approved, in slightly amended versions, by the Constitutional Tribunal of the State.

Linguistic Normalisation

Generally speaking, linguistic normalisation can be viewed as a success in all three regions, especially with regard to language development and the production of linguistic tools, as well as the setting up of education programmes. In all three Autonomous Communities different models of immersion programmes exist, with a growing number of children attending classes where the medium of instruction is not Castilian Spanish. The vehicle for higher education, particularly in university courses in the humanities, is now increasingly in the region's own language, as far as both Catalonia and the Basque Country are concerned. In Catalonia, local and regional government business, as well as most legal and administrative matters, are normally transacted in Catalan. They can be carried out in both the local language and Spanish in the Basque region and also, to a lesser extent, in Galicia. In terms of status planning, normalisation can be said to be more controversial, as it involves many different and competing pressures. This is a point I shall come back to later.

The planning and implementation of language policies has, naturally, also encountered innumerable problems. On the more practical side there are those related to resources. Promotion of the regional language is a costly exercise in terms of the production of materials, training of teachers, administrators, people employed in the media. And then there are problems which cannot be resolved however much money is being poured into the exercise. To a large extent they stem from the traditional opposition in Spain, mainly by Castilians, to the territorial solution of linguistic conflict. Opposition is voiced most forcefully by the *españolistas*, who try to defend what they see as the linguistic rights of immigrants and state officials. As a result of the constitutional acceptance of territoriality, Castilians are now expected to adapt linguistically to the linguistic situation of the region in which they live, whereas previously they could just use Castilian wherever they were. Comet i Codina (1990), in fact, considers the obstacles to linguistic normalisation to be 'tremendous' and 'enormous', and he blames 'historical inertia, the sheer fact of uniformism having lasted so long' (1990: 112) in particular. This is noticeable in attitudes demonstrated by people with vested interests, especially civil servants (in Spain a large number of professions, like teaching, health service etc. fall under the category of *funcionarios públicos*) who resist learning and using the regional language.

Catalonia

Before dealing with the issue of language and identity in Spain, I will look briefly at some of the results of linguistic normalisation in the three autonomous communities. Catalonia's first Law of Linguistic Normalisation (of April 1983) is the most explicit. Catalan linguistic policy aims ostensibly at achieving a situation where there is 'equality of both languages'. This would, of course involve 'equal bilingualism'. But given the huge advantage Castilian has always enjoyed, language policies tend to concentrate on the exclusive promotion of Catalan with the objective of giving it a high profile and expanding its knowledge and use among those who live in Catalonia. This has been discussed by many writers on the subject (e.g. Vallverdú, 1979, 1981; Hoffmann, 1988, 1991; Fishman, 1991).

In education, for instance, the implied assumption is that bilingualism is to be considered a transitory stage until all education can be carried out through the medium of Catalan. The sociolinguistic preconditions were reasonably favourable for such aims. The Catalan language had been standardised at the beginning of the century, it had already started to be used in education and, most importantly, it had a large number of users among the influential members of the middle classes who were enthusiastic about promoting it.

An overwhelming proportion of Catalans in Catalonia have supported their local government's linguistic policies, which were introduced at a time when they were eager for change. An interesting point to note is that there seemed to exist a possible relationship between political and linguistic behaviour in Catalonia, which the Austrian linguist, Karl Ille, examined on the basis of election results from 1977–1986 and published in 1988. He was able to point to a close correlation between support for nationalist parties, both on the political right and the left, on the one hand, and fluency coupled with frequency of use on the other. In other words, Catalans expressed their identity and their wishes for their country through both language and voting patterns.

Only when one takes into account the large number of immigrants of non-Catalan background and examines their attitudes towards the language policies of the Generalitat (the Catalan autonomous government) does it become obvious that not all of Catalonia's inhabitants are equally enthusiastic about galloping catalanisation. Since public life is now almost entirely carried out in Catalan, some have argued (e.g. Mar-Molinero, 1990) that as far as Castilian-speaking immigrants are concerned a reverse form of diglossia exists, with Catalan the High form and Castilian (usually a non-standard variety of it) as the Low. To what extent these immigrants feel linguistically discriminated against is perhaps another matter. No doubt many of them feel socially disadvantaged as they often come from a low socioeconomic background and live in poor housing areas, often in large, homogenous groups. For everyday purposes they probably do not need to use Catalan although, of course, they may resent being made to feel in a linguistically inferior position. However, this does not mean that attitudes are totally negative, as witnessed, for instance, by Woolard's extensive studies (e.g. 1989).

Against this background, it is interesting to consider the tone and some of the provisions of the New Law of Linguistic Normalisation (1994). The reason why it was thought necessary to have a new Law was that the use of Catalan (all the following translations are mine) 'had not advanced sufficiently in some areas'; other factors taken into account were the linguistic development of Catalan society (with a new generation of young people who have gone right through the educational system, and therefore been educated in Catalan, now seeking work; and also in view of the fact that 'almost the whole population of Catalonia understands Catalan and is highly competent in the use of the language') and the experience gained since 1983. The intention of the New Law is stated quite clearly: 'to reinforce the linguistic rights of the citizens of Catalonia' — by guaranteeing, for example, that staff in public administration will both (1) know Catalan and (2) answer in Catalan (the 1983 Law only guaranteed the right to speak to them in this language). To this end, Article 2 establishes Catalan as 'the language of *normal* use in public administration, and in the educational system; and in the communications and information which private bodies address to the public' (my emphasis). The Preamble says explicitly that the aim is to increase the use of the language in Catalan society, so as to put Catalan on an equal footing with any other 'own language' used in its territory — 'without prejudice to the rights and duties derived from the official status of Castilian Spanish' (the new Law continues the guarantee that citizens will be entitled to use both official languages and that all children will acquire both Catalan and Spanish).

The following examples of provisions contained in the Law, however, leave little doubt (in view of both their general thrust and their actual content) as to the real aspirations of Catalans: Article 2 says that knowledge of Catalan will be a requirement for obtaining a post in public administration; Article 15 lays down that the School Leaving Certificate (without which it is not possible to apply for a job anywhere in Spain) will not be issued to school leavers unable to demonstrate the appropriate knowledge of Catalan; Article 16 states that the use of Catalan 'as the normal vehicle of expression' is guaranteed in higher education, and Article 18 specifies that both school and university teachers (but not visiting professors!) must have 'sufficient knowledge' of Catalan.

Article 21 mentions *acciones de fomento*, which can be interpreted as some kind of 'positive action' (in Article 23 they are actually called *medidas positivas de actuación*), such as positive discrimination in the granting of subsidies. As far as use of Catalan in the media is concerned, Article 23 says that Catalan must be the language normally used in the media, including publicity, and it introduces minimum quotas for Catalan radio programmes and for films in Catalan or with Catalan subtitles (radio and cinema are a responsibility of the Generalitat — as national television is controlled by the central government, all the new Law says is that TV programmes must contribute to the normalisation of Catalan in accordance with state legislation). Notice, however, that 'obligatory quotas' must not demand more than 50% 'presence of Catalan' in the relevant activity — which makes one wonder if there is some kind of contradiction here: is 'normal' more than one half, or is it less?

Public and private firms, according to Article 24, must within two years use Catalan *en la rotulación* (public signs, headings, lettering and titles) addressed to the public, even if they use Spanish as well; and firms which enjoy 'administrative concessions' from the Generalitat or any other Catalan authorities must use Catalan (again, not necessarily in exclusivity) in their adverts, labels, circulars, documentation, publicity etc. Finally, sanctions are specified for non-compliance: Article 29 states that it will be an 'administrative infringement' (*infracción administrativa*, which sounds very much like 'a civil offence') to obstruct or ignore the Law or not to keep to the minimum quotas. 'Infringements' will be classified as either 'slight' or 'serious', which will be sanctioned under the authority of the Director General of Language Policy, or as 'very serious' and punished by the Councillor in charge of cultural affairs. If the Director General of Language Policy is a language planner, which is possible (it has happened in the past), it may be one of the few times in history when a linguist is able to impose fines for a linguistic offence!

One unexpected Castilian reaction to the New Law (and of course to the whole linguistic situation developing in Catalonia) was that in October 1994 the Director of the *Real Academia Española de la Lengua* wrote to the Prime Minister asking for measures to protect Spanish in the bilingual Autonomous Communities. The Generalitat's answer was that this venerable institution 'knows nothing at all' about the *realidad lingüística de Cataluña* (see *El País* issues of 10, 12 and 21 November 1994).

Euskadi

In contrast to the other two autonomous regions, the geographical area where Basque is spoken today has diminished considerably over the course of history. Thus, the demise of Basque has been accelerated by the interplay of three major determinants: loss of territory, immigration and oppression by the central government. A number of other factors, social and linguistic ones, such as the lack of a standardised form of Basque and a restricted social infrastructure of native speakers, have also contributed towards language shift.

Because of the prevailing social and political conditions in the Basque country, linguistic normalisation has had to proceed at a much slower pace. It has also been a much more complex process. Apart from a few early texts from the Middle Ages, Basque has no written literary tradition, although it does possess a very strong oral one. Basque had never been used for administrative or educational purposes, and therefore a generally agreed standard variety did not exist. Traditionally, Basque was spoken in rural areas by less well-educated people, and for this reason it acquired low social prestige even among its own speakers. In addition, Basque had, over the years of suppression, become closely associated with political radicalism.

Basque finally became standardised by the late 1960s, but differences of agreement on linguistic norms still remain. The standard form that has been decided upon is called *euskera batúa* or *vasco normalizado* (two spellings are used: *euskera* and *euskara*). It appears to be based on educated Guipuzkoa Basque, and it is not always accepted by those who speak other varieties — for example, speakers of Bizkaia Basque, for whom it is almost a new language (Badía, 1987). It is not easy to increase the number of Basque speakers (at present only about 600,000, or approximately a quarter of the population of Euskadi), and thus the number of possible teachers of the language, as Basque is a difficult language to learn. It has been suggested that something like 300–500 hours of teaching are required in order to achieve a reasonable knowledge of the language (Hooper, 1995). A further obstacle lies in the fact that, in contrast to Galician and Catalan, there is no degree of mutual intelligibility with Castilian. In addition, as already explained, in the Basque-Navarrese area there are as many as seven vernaculars (some used by very few people) which are said to be mutually unintelligible. Whereas individual efforts are geared towards promoting Basque, or rather the unified norm of *euskera batúa*, giving it a higher profile and enabling more people to have access to it (in primary, secondary and adult education programmes), the overall goal is to achieve bilingualism and to foster more positive attitudes towards Basque, both on the part of those who already speak it and those who are possible learners of the language.

The link between language and identity is a more complex phenomenon in the Basque country. On the one hand, there is no shortage of authorities who assert that there is a close interrelation between the two. This is enshrined in the Statute of Autonomy and in the Law of Normalisation of the Use of Basque. Roger Collins (not a linguist) examines a number of different criteria according to which

Basque national identity can be established. He accepts that their exceptionally long history has helped to provide a focus for national identity, but he says that this identity cannot be defined either in physical or in material cultural terms. 'This then leaves language as the sole satisfactory tool with which it is possible to approach the question of Basque identity and origins' (Collins, 1986: 8). Others point to the fact that a Basque defines himself in terms of language when he calls himself an *euskaldun*, which means someone who possesses *euskara*, in the same way as the name for the Basque Country, *Euskal-herri*, means the land of the Basque language (Allières, 1985, quoted in Comet i Codina, 1990).

On the other hand, there are undoubtedly many Basques who identify fully with Basqueness although they do not speak the language. On the part of many, perhaps the majority, in Euskadi there is a strong commitment to a Basque cultural and ethnic identity and a belief in territorial integrity. Language may in many settings be the most important factor in deciding identity, but ethnicity and a claim to a territory are key identifying characteristics, too (Wardhaugh, 1987). In the case of the Basques, identity seems to be based primarily on descent and self-identification, with language playing an additional, but not decisive, role. This view can be supported by the findings of Ille's study of language and political behaviour. Ille (1988) shows that, whereas the backing of Basque nationalist parties has, in general, grown over the years, they have always received proportionally more support from non-Basque speakers than from Basque-speaking voters. He concludes that Basque identity goes far beyond linguistic identity.

The absence of a traditionally Basque-speaking middle class has also made the task of linguistic normalisation more difficult. Geographical, socioeconomic and political factors account for the fact that the majority of the Basque Country remained a rural society for many centuries. But it is one of the clearest signs that things are changing for the better, as far as the Basque language is concerned, that in an otherwise still quite precarious situation marked by language decline, there now seems to be a growing number of middle-class speakers of *euskera*, as well as many parents who take an interest in their children's education in Basque, which makes the regional distribution of speakers of the language less patchy.

It is true that the overall number of speakers who habitually speak Basque has not expanded greatly as a result of linguistic normalisation, but the number of those who now possess reading and writing skills in the language has increased, whereas in the past most users just had oral competence. In fact, some writers on the subject consider the use of Basque in education the area where language planning efforts in Euskadi are the most tangible and promising (Cobarrubias & Garmendia, 1987, for example). And the linguistic behaviour of Basque speakers has changed: they now use their own language in more diverse social contexts than ever before. This, together with the language promotion efforts made by many different institutions, has contributed to an improvement in the perceived social status of Basque.

Galicia

Several of the trends just outlined are discernible, too, in Galicia. However, as has been mentioned before, the linguistic history of, and the present sociolinguistic situation in, that part of Spain are really quite different from those of the other regions, so that comparisons are not very useful. Indeed, the application of the same model of linguistic normalisation may prove to have been something of a costly academic exercise with only limited success.

The diglossic relationship of Galician and Castilian Spanish has persisted for a long time, Galician being the popular, widespread vehicle for oral communication. In the past Castilian was the language used in and by the administration, schools, the media, military service and most other walks of public life; it also was the only medium for written communication. Galician had little association with the arts and the intelligentsia, and no history of having been the language of official public use.

Before 1978 there were one or two brief periods when there was some literary output in Galician, but on the whole this language did not have a strong and influential literary tradition to look back on (for most people in Spain, the only known writer in Galician is Rosalía de Castro, a poet of the 19th century, even if they are aware that several better known authors from Alfonso the Wise in the 13th century to Lorca in the 20th who, just like Rosalía de Castro, wrote mainly in Castilian Spanish but from time to time also in Galician, especially poetry). However, there was a tradition of nationalism in Galicia going back to the end of the 19th century, which may not have been as strong, or as forcefully expressed, as in Catalonia, but was nevertheless real enough for Galicians; and during the Second Spanish Republic nationalist sentiments and the *Partido Galleguista* succeeded in getting parliament to approve a Statute of Autonomy with wide powers for the region in June 1936. Unfortunately, the Spanish Civil War started three weeks later, so it was never put into effect — but of course that (as it happened, overwhelming) vote in favour of autonomy endowed later efforts in the same direction with as much historical justification as was claimed by the other two *autonomías históricas*.

When the programme of linguistic normalisation in Galicia was set into motion the first task was to find an acceptable standard variety. The absence of an already agreed upon standard naturally slowed down the pace at which linguistic policies could be implemented. There was no obvious candidate to chose from among the three main Galician dialects, which also contain sub-varieties. Codification and development of the language were complicated by the existence of two language 'camps', one, the *lusistas* or *reintegrationists*, favouring a closer alignment with Portuguese (with which Galician is unquestionably related), arguing that 'Galician's best chance of being culturally effective' (Willis, 1992: 7) lay in its reintegration with a major language such as Portuguese. The other, the *independists*, argued for an independent development of Galician, that is, independent from both Castilian and Portuguese.

There also exists a bastardised form of Galician, known as *castrapo*, which can be seen as a further Galician dialect characterised by the heavy influence of Castilian. The existence and widespread use of *castrapo* has always made it difficult to be sure about the exact number of Galician speakers. It is claimed that 99% of Galicia's 2.8 million citizens understand Galician and that some 80% speak it (Willis, 1992). Hooper (1995) cites a 1990 Spanish government survey which puts the number of Galicians who speak Galician 'well' at 63%, compared with a figure of 68% for Catalan and 26% for Basque.

The *Instituto da Lingua Galega* published their linguistic norms, covering orthography and morphology, even before the Law of Linguistic Normalisation was passed, and immediately these were opposed by the other camp, which proposed a different set of norms, claiming that the new ones conceded too much to Castilian with regard both to spelling and also pronunciation — in addition to making it into a kind of scholars' language, rather than one that could be easily taught in schools. The upshot of these disputes has been that Galician now appears to have, not one agreed set of orthographic rules, but two or even three systems (the third being one which was published by a subgroup of the *lusistas*, who used the 1986 spelling reforms proposed for Portuguese), which apparently are not always kept separate (Willis, 1992). Today the *independists* seem to be in the majority and in more influential positions, for instance in the *Real Academia Galega* and the *Instituto da Lingua Galega*, where the official decisions on matters of language are made, and they are also represented in Galicia's main publishing house.

Disagreements of this sort do little to persuade those who already speak a dialect variety of Galician to accept the officially-promoted version as the prestigious norm.

Corpus planning is evidently of great importance in Galicia, but so is status planning (the 'dignification' of Galician, as Comet i Codina, 1990, calls it). Continued language use is dependent on a number of usually interrelated factors — locality, social background and age of speakers being among the most important. In the case of Galician there is a notable absence of positive correlation between these factors and language use: on the contrary, Galician is most commonly spoken among the older, lower-class rural population. Hooper makes what is perhaps a sweeping generalisation when he says that whereas Catalan is '"the language of the people" in the sense that it is spoken in every stratum of society, Galician is the language of the people in the sense that it is spoken by the "masses"' (1995: 420). It is true that there are very high rates of Galician–Castilian bilingualism, which is facilitated by the marked degree of mutual intelligibility between the two languages. However, this bilingualism tends to be asymmetrical, i.e. diglossic. It is not balanced bilingualism acquired in early childhood, as Castilian Spanish tends to be learned only through education and contact with the media, whereas Galician is usually the first language acquired but not further developed through education. In addition, most speakers, when they use Galician throughout their lives, do so merely for oral interaction.

Therefore, because of its association with the older and rural population, and hence its traditionally low prestige, language policies promoting Galician have to be targeted at young, urban, middle-class speakers — the very groups who, as a result of migration, upward social mobility and increased exposure to education and the media, contribute towards language decline. The government's provisions for language promotion have, of course, been designed for the whole population. However, urban and rural Galicians are affected by them in different ways, and it does not seem clear that galicianisation will be guaranteed. Nor does it seem totally justified to talk about normalisation in terms of the interpretation offered earlier, that is, restoration of a previously-existing situation.

In 1973 Alonso Montero, a Galician linguist, published a book (a dramatic report, he called it) in which he voiced his fears for the future survival of Galician and outlined the many problems affecting the language. In a new version published in 1991 he is much more positive, although he warns of new problems with which the language is now besieged. Generally, on the positive side a number of achievements can be listed: a norm has been found and is being disseminated at a fast rate through the media (less successfully by television than by radio or in the press), the educational system and positive action by local and regional authorities, with the goodwill and cooperation of most of Galicia's inhabitants. Also, in terms of changing attitudes, linguistic normalisation has been successful as is shown by a series of surveys into language proficiency and attitudes reported by Monteagudo & Santamarina (1993). But what about success in the sense of restoring Galician to a position where it is normal to use it in all situations? Such a 'normal situation' never did exist. So, although Galician language planners talk about *linguistic normalisation*, this does not seem a realistic aim. However, it is probably true to say that there were times in Galicia's history when Galician was less socially stigmatised and seen more positively as a symbol of Galician identity.

Castilian Spanish always played an important role as the standard and prestige variety, just as Galicia's dialects fulfilled their role in everyday communication and as reinforcers of a regional identity which the Galicians, too, see mainly in terms of ethnic distinctiveness. Linguistic normalisation has now brought the urban population (who have always been Castilian-speaking) into contact with a language which is being promoted vigorously by their government and has been endowed with positive attributes, e.g. embodying Galicianess. *Gallego normalizado* (that is, Galician standardised on the basis of the *norma urbana culta* (or educated standard urban Galician) is quite easy to learn for Spanish speakers because of its many similarities with Castilian and, I suspect, also because for many it is a matter of acquiring it passively since there is no real need to use it actively unless one wants to be employed in the region's administration or education system. It also seems to be the case that most children who learn Galician in school and study part of their school curriculum through the medium of Galician do not end up being habitual users of the language. This may lead one to think that middle-class support for Galician has primarily a political motivation, the need to maintain (and be seen to maintain) one's cultural heritage upon which political autonomy is founded.

And what about those who have always spoken Galician? On one hand the traditional strength Galician has always enjoyed in the countryside is being eroded as a result of changed lifestyles, migration etc. But whether those who are affected by this kind of language loss, or replacement, actually mind has not been the subject of any inquiry that I know of. On the other hand, these speakers now find that their dialect variety risks becoming a liability as it does not conform to the standard that is being promoted, which represents a superimposed variety. Having to accept and acquire literacy in this new form may well be perceived as an alienating element. Culturally, it is probably hard for them to recognise *gallego normalizado* as part of their heritage. Yet not accepting it bears some risk, too. Social mobility and migration (both into urban areas and through urban sprawl into the countryside) bring with them increased contact with Castilian Spanish as well as with the new Standard Galician. Which variety should one acquire? One thing seems sure: constant contact with these two varieties will remind rural speakers that they use neither of them well — and this 'not speaking well' is an old, well-known complex they have had to live with for generations. So now the situation is even more difficult than before for them. As John Green so poignantly comments, it is a repetition of the old situation of 'conflict diglossia'. Again, it is the middle-class who determines language policy (the new emerging galician-ised one), but this time there may be more antagonism caused, although this is far from being what the language planners intended. 'In particular', Green writes, 'the chances of conflict are increased if rural speakers feel they are placed in double linguistic jeopardy or denied access, by redefined educational priorities, to the effective instruction in Castilian that would still offer a passport to social mobility' (1994: 165).

The Debate on National Identity

Official language planning efforts in Spain over the last 20 years have been paralleled by an ongoing public debate in the Spanish quality press. In terms of both who the participants are and its intensity and general tenor, the debate has been quite striking at times, at least for the non-Spanish observer. The writers of articles such as the ones I shall mention in a moment (linguists, academics and well-known writers) are people who elsewhere in Europe would perhaps take part in polemics in daily newspapers less frequently, if at all; and the arguments they put forward, as well as the conclusions that they come to, are often quite extraordinary. Many of these contributions have dealt with issues of bilingualism and identity; and the impact that they have on public opinion and personal attitudes must be regarded as quite considerable, to judge from the number of other articles and letters to the editor which appear almost every week, and also from the heat with which people of all persuasions and social groups argue over such topics in ordinary conversation.

The first article that I have chosen is one of the most extraordinary among the many that I have seen. It is entitled 'Signs of Identity' (a reference to the novel *Señas de identidad*, Mexico 1966, by the Spanish author Juan Goytisolo, which was arguably the most influential work of fiction of the Franco period). The article in question was written by a professor of linguistics at the University of Barcelona, Jesús Tusón, and published in the national daily *El País* in 1988. The author begins by stating that the vast majority of the world's inhabitants are *mono*lingual and that bilinguals, if they exist at all, are much nearer to monolingualism than to linguistic diversity (*sic*). He argues that one should seriously doubt whether there are any real bilinguals anywhere, that is, people who can 'move spontaneously and with the same ease in two languages'. 'The usual thing', he goes on, 'in those whom we consider bilinguals is that they move spontaneously and with complete ease in one language, and besides this they know another language to a varying degree of competence' — and they use each language in different contexts or sets of circumstances. Tusón then describes what he calls *el bilingüe* *ideal* and of course he claims that such a person does not exist: 'If anyone comes very near our ideal bilingual, he must certainly be 'a white blackbird' (*un mirlo blanco* or one in a million; he is not the only one in Catalonia who believes that bilingualism is a myth: see, for instance, the sociolinguist Aracil 1973). This kind of argument reflects the way many Spaniards, including specialists in linguistics, either confuse or choose to disregard such elementary concepts as bilingualism and ambilingualism at the outset of the debate. Tusón believes that the so-called multilingual states are all going through intermediate stages leading inevitably to national monolingualism (in the national official language, to be sure), because, in his view, 'a language is that which has the support of the army, the navy and the air force'. From such extreme premises Tusón draws equally fascinating conclusions. He cites the situation of Catalan in France, which is disappearing under the onslaught of the powerful French state, and he suggests that the only possible remedy is 'an energetic language defence policy' (*una política de enérgica defensa de la lengua autóctona*), implying that the only way to defend Catalan in Catalonia properly is to gear towards this end a vigorous action using the resources of the national (i.e. Catalan) powers. (Actually, this is not a bad description of what public authorities have done and are still doing in the Principality.) Tusón ends his article with a twist, in view of the ideas he has already put forward: in the Europe of the future *every one* of its languages must be valued and protected, since each constitutes, not only an essential part of our cultural heritage, but also the most precious sign of our identity.

This last remark demonstrates a frequently-voiced sentiment in contemporary Spain, namely, the feeling that the age-old conflicts between centre and periphery can somehow be solved within the wider framework of a Europe of the Nations. On the question of 'ideal bilingualism', it is perhaps somewhat ironic to observe that Catalonia must be one of the places in the world with most ambilinguals — because of factors such as the similarities between Catalan and Spanish and also because most adult Catalans were educated in Spanish but have used both languages extensively during the last 20 years; and yet there is little doubt that very many of these practising ambilinguals identify themselves firmly as Catalan. It becomes clear from this kind of debate, I think, that bilingualism and identity are separate issues and should be treated as such.

Next I will refer to an article by another linguistics professor from the same university, which was published in a prestigious critical book review journal, *Saber Leer*, in 1987. In it Antoni Badía i Margarit (now President of the *Institut d'Estudis Catalans*) deals quite extensively and informatively with the language situation in Spain at that time, and he expresses attitudes towards linguistic policies which are quite representative of catalanistas and defenders of the interest of Catalonia's language. Badía makes three points which are relevant in this context — and range from the generally acceptable to the contentious. First, that it is right that regional language policies in the Spanish Autonomous Communities which are officially bilingual should be geared to 'pay attention to the languages in danger of being forgotten'. Second, that there is no linguistic discrimination against non-Catalans in Catalonia because Catalan language laws are not statutes establishing linguistic 'territoriality', i.e. compulsory use of a language within a territory, as are, for instance, Belgian laws. In Catalonia, it is the non-Catalan immigrants themselves who demand to be taught Catalan. And thirdly, he vigorously denies that it could be justified to speak about 'language disloyalty' in Spain. This concept has been used by Gregorio Salvador (1983) in polemical writing criticising Castilian speakers who neglect or abandon their own language or acquire that of their adoptive place of residence. The fact that this kind of argument can arise in the first place again demonstrates the Spaniards' unease with the phenomenon of bilingualism (and, perhaps, the inevitable requirement of compromise that it entails). With regard to the results of Catalan language policies, Badía points to a number of shortcomings, some of which have now been addressed by the New Normalisation Law.

A third position in the debate on language planning and issues of identity is the one taken by many of the *españolistas* who fear for the position of Castilian Spanish in the new Spain. Many people (not just the Director of the *Real Academia*) complain about the effect that the emphasis on regional languages is having on the national language, Castilian Spanish. An article published in the prestigious Madrid newspaper *El País* on 11 April, 1991, by the popular novelist Francisco Ayala, who also happens to be a member of the Royal Academy, may serve as an example.

Spanish society, Ayala claims, is suffering from a linguistic 'boomerang effect': the previously-repressed non-Castilian languages of Spain 'are being imposed by force' (although, as he says, the majority of the population in the autonomous regions of Spain do not actually know the local language) by arrogant people with old-fashioned nationalist ideas who are now in power in the Autonomous Communities, who are trying to 'push out' Spanish from their territories. He says that 'Spanish has fallen into neglect', not only in the self-governing periphery, but all over the country, and this is noticed by visiting Latin Americans who say that they now feel more pride in their Spanish language than Spaniards do. It should be a thing of the past to believe that there is any kind of connection between language and national character, but clearly in contemporary Spain many people emphasise their non-Spanish language as a way of affirming their nationalistic allegiance. The correct attitude, Ayala maintains, would be one of 'civilised respect and even-tempered acceptance of linguistic plurality', without trying to impose the use of any language on reluctant users. Although one may sympathise with the suggestion that Ayala makes at the end, the one-sided and ill-informed manner in which he argues reveals that the linguistic debate is not a representation of well-considered argument.

This mixture of good sense and exaggeration is noticeable also in an article by a young writer, Enrique Olmos, published in *El País* fairly recently (on 4 November, 1994).

Nationalism, Olmos says, is a thing of the past. Today it is perfectly possible to identify oneself as both a Basque, say, a Spaniard, a European and a citizen of the world. This means that there is now scarcely any need to accept or require any kind of national component in the person's feelings of identity, and in fact one's nationality (i.e. ascription or allegiance to a national or ethnic group — not 'nationality' in the narrow sense of 'citizenship') can be freely chosen without contradicting identity in any way. This was not possible in the past, when there were very considerable communication barriers. What has changed is that there is now wide use of supra-national languages in the world. In the new situation, the encouragement of societal multilingualism in places like the Spanish bilingual Autonomous Communities is less significant than it used to be. Olmos puts forward the idea that, in fact, the Spanish self-governing regions which do *not* have their own local language may enjoy a potential advantage — it may be easier for them to develop bilingualism in Spanish and another important world language (for instance, English), presumably because resources can be concentrated. Present-day language conflict in some parts of the bilingual communities in Spain may even be resented by future generations, for the following reason: achieving individual bilingualism or multilingualism that includes one of the world languages (he must have English in mind here) may continue to be possible exclusively for the members of socially-privileged classes (for example, the children of middle-class parents in Catalonia), but those coming from socially-disadvantaged groups, who now have no means to acquire important languages, may realise soon that they are unable to compete professionally on equal terms in the world (and the Europe) of tomorrow. Olmos warns against this 'historical fraud' and maintains that it is 'an aberration' to encourage 'local, but quite unimportant, languages' (*lenguas locales de escaso alcance*). It is of course difficult to see how this kind of argument could be backed up by research on second and subsequent language learning in schools.

The importance of feelings of identity in contemporary Spanish society is seen even more clearly in an article by another Barcelona professor, Victor Gomez Pin, published in *El País* in 1994, an article which is a blistering attack against the prevalent linguistic intransigence evidenced, according to the author, by many Catalans, Basques and others in today's Spain. I think that this article reflects important conflicts that are often referred to in everyday conversation among Spaniards nowadays.

Gómez Pin says that some people in Catalonia have such strong anti-Spanish feelings that they are even reluctant to use the word 'Spain', and they prefer to say 'the Spanish state' (*el Estado español*) instead. The reason for this is that there are many people in, say, Barcelona or San Sebastian, who do not consider themselves (or these cities) to be Spanish at all. These people accept the legality of their 'Spanish citizenship', but they define their own identity as purely Catalan/Basque/etc. and non-Spanish, i.e. they *declare*, but do not *recognise*, themselves as Spanish. As a consequence, many others in the rest of Spain appear to have adopted by now a new feeling of Spanish identity in which part of the definition is also negative (that is, non-Catalan, non-Basque, etc). So instead of mutual *recognition* there is mutual *repudiation* leading to resentment, in which there is loss of dignity on both sides. (Gómez Pin calls it *dignity*, and his article is entitled *La dignidad de España*; I think that this idea can be related to the old Spanish concept of *honour*, which has a very long tradition in Spanish culture.)

Gómez Pin goes on to say that Catalans and others who claim that their own identity cannot be properly (he actually says 'with proper dignity') defined except by excluding their links with the rest of Spain lay themselves open to what he calls an 'irrefutable' argument, namely that, if these links are forced on them, and therefore they are *legal* but not *legitimate*, it is not dignified to accept them in any way at all. It is not a dignified thing to do, he claims, to demand of those who do not *identify* themselves as Spaniards that they should *declare* themselves to be Spanish; and, correspondingly, the only proper thing for them to do is to accept as Spanish exclusively those who *do* identify themselves as such. The same applies to the acceptance of the languages: what the author refers to as *el estatuto de hispanohablante* (i.e. recognised status as a native speaker of Spanish) should be respected, not despised, by those who not long ago, and in the name of official Spanish orthodoxy, were themselves oppressed because of their allegiance to their own linguistic identity.

Judging from these kinds of arguments, it seems that 'identity' more often than not is seen in terms of collective, rather than individual feelings; that is, to some extent it is a case of identification by others rather than self-ascription. There always appear to be just two choices, or perhaps a dilemma: seeing oneself either as Spanish, on the one hand, or on the other as Catalan/Basque etc. It will be interesting to see whether after another decade of *de facto* bilingualism and adjustment to the new Spanish territorial divisions, a new type of bilingual–bicultural identity will emerge.

Conclusion

Language planning in democratic Spain has been a major pillar of the Autonomous Communities' political and cultural programmes. In all three regions examined here it has resulted in qualitative improvements for the languages concerned. An impressive number of dictionaries, grammars, orthographical guidelines and terminological guides have been produced, and learned bodies have been set up, entrusted with the development and dissemination of the newly elevated languages. We, as linguists, can only be full of admiration (and envy at the amount of money made available for linguistic work). However, the challenge of winning over all potential users of these languages has yet not been won.

From the point of reversing language shift one is also left with a degree of optimism, however uneven. In Fishman's comprehensive treatment of language shift, Catalonia's efforts to restore its language are counted among the success stories. Fishman highlights the increased acceptance of the use of Catalan among Catalan speakers, even in 'mixed company', and he points towards the growing number of speakers who today use their own language when previously they would have used Castilian Spanish, e.g. teachers, politicians, TV and radio announcers etc. He no longer sees Catalan to be diminishing in uses and users: 'indeed, there is good reason to conclude that it [Catalan] is moving ahead on both fronts and in both of the target groups that it must keep in mind' (1991: 323).

On the other hand, Fishman still counts Basque among the threatened languages. Despite all the efforts that have been made, the difficulties deriving from the small number of mother-tongue speakers, the lack of widely-perceived importance for expressing Basque identity through language, the problems surrounding an overall acceptable standard form, and the fact that it is often not transmitted from parents to their children as a language of the home — all these are powerful obstacles standing in the way of reversing language shift in the Basque Country and of increasing the number of its speakers. Partial success has been achieved in that the process of language decline has been slowed down, as those who previously only had oral competence in the language may now have full competence in it, and the language seems to have gained in prestige as public administration and education have embraced bilingualism, while in some areas of public life Basque has become fully established.

It is obviously early days for an assessment of other, perhaps more permanent, changes in patterns of linguistic behaviour and attitudes in Spain as a whole. Certainly among many who work in the central administration of the state, either in Madrid or for Madrid in the regions, attitudes towards the regional languages still tend to be unfavourable. Comet i Codina is quite pessimistic about a change of linguistic attitudes in Spain when he predicts that it will probably still be a long time before: (a) all Spanish-speaking schoolchildren are taught dispassionately about the cultural and linguistic diversity of their country; and (b) until one can detect a change in the mental outlook of the linguistic majority — about which he says: 'For this linguistic majority, it is a firm and unalterable belief that, while the Castilian-speaking area is the domain of a single language, Castilian speakers have the divine right to be linguistically at home in the whole country' (1990: 112).

For the time being, it seems to be clear that the eagerness of the bilingual Autonomous Communities to promote their own languages has led to the adoption of a particular model of language planning, the Catalan one, and this has meant that the orientation and formulation of language policies in Galicia and (to a lesser extent) in the Basque Country have also been overshadowed by the Catalan experience. This 'copycat factor' has begun to have undesirable effects, even if pursuing such policies in the first place may have been historically justified and politically opportune. But it is becoming evident that linguistic action has not always been matched by sociolinguistic good sense or sensibility. This has created problems in Galicia, as we have seen, and also in Catalonia itself.

There is no doubt that the language policies of the Catalan Generalitat have wide popular support, which is shown consistently in opinion polls and in surveys carried out by newspapers and magazines. If Catalans are asked, they always show favourable attitudes towards the recovery of Catalan. But they are much more guarded about the advantages of bilingualism, which many see as a potential source of conflict (see for example, the opinions expressed by a group of students and professional people reported in the magazine *El Ciervo* in 1987. The same kind of ambivalence can be observed in others, e.g. Tovar (1982), Rojo (1982), Fernández-Sevilla (1986).

The push for catalanisation came from, and was supported by, the Catalan élite who, of course, stood to gain most. It appears that among the Catalan lower classes the Catalan language has also been supported because it offers a means of upward social mobility and provides something of a 'feelgood factor' — after all, Catalan is supposed to be the language of all Catalans. But by this very claim those who live in Catalonia but do not see themselves as Catalans, nor aspire to become Catalans, can feel patronised, even minoritised. Non-Catalans constitute a sizeable new minority in Catalonia, and this section of its population is likely, to continue to increase proportionately to the total number of inhabitants, as already pointed out.

Fishman seems to assume that the problem of non-Catalan speakers may be solved with time, as he suggests that 'before the ultimate goal can be attained, a new "reverse diglossia" will have to be at least transitionally attained, with Catalan H and Spanish L' (1991: 313). I doubt whether this is a likely scenario, at any rate for as long as Catalonia remains a constituent part of Spain. Castilian Spanish is, after all, the national language, it is widely used everywhere and it remains prominent throughout Catalonia itself. Catalans need to understand and speak Spanish, whereas most non-Catalan Spaniards do not need to know Catalan. Therefore, linguistic normalisation of Spanish native speakers resident in Catalonia will only be achieved if attitudes in the rest of Spain are positive towards Spanish-Catalan bilingualism. As we have seen, at the moment such a situation does not prevail. This is the basic challenge of the future for linguistic normalisation in Catalonia.

The linguist Jacob Mey (1989), writing from a sociopolitical position about language politics, is a good deal more critical than Fishman. For him language planning is a form of social control, as it aims to manipulate people's language use. Within this framework he argues that normalisation (which he describes as linguistic upgrading) has been a process whereby the norm has been decided, as he says, 'top-down'. Implementation of language policies is carried out by 'culture workers', who too often ignore individual language users. Thus, pointing towards the discrepancy between the ways the Catalan government likes to represent Catalonia as being Catalan, and the way all those who do not speak Catalan but live in Catalonia see themselves, he describes the situation in terms of 'conflict diglossia'. He concludes his article by warning that language planners in Catalonia are running the risk of reproducing and cementing the very structures they were supposed to do away with, namely the oppression of social or ethnic minorities by the dominant majority. By promoting one language for all and claiming that Catalan is the language of all Catalans, they are doing the same as Franco did when he came to power and promoted Castilian. Even though this claim may be considered to be somewhat exaggerated, I think that it does contain more than a grain of truth. It certainly provides the critics of language planning with ammunition.

In Galicia, too, a similar reversal of roles has been observed, although there the task at hand in language planning is a different one. The Castilian-speaking middle-class speakers must be won round to the new Galician standard, and so must the traditional lower-class dialect speakers. In other words, Galician must be turned into a vehicle of social advancement, and to achieve this end linguistic behaviour and the linguistic situation have to be changed by artificial means. But why should such manoeuvres be successful, if there is no real communicative need to change one's linguistic behaviour in the first place? One can also say, viewing the issue from a different perspective, that it is difficult to see how language change initiated from above can be as successful as change emerging from below.

It seems to me that language planning in Spain has reached a point where its goals, as well as its policies, need to be reconsidered and their goals readjusted so as to meet different local requirements. How far should language maintenance measures be pursued? What kind of language promotion can count on wide popular support? What should the priorities be? Would the promotion of widespread, and institutionalised, bilingualism (with equal emphasis on both languages) not lead to a more acceptable form of *convivencia* and true linguistic pluralism *now*, and would it not be worth paying the price of an increased risk of long-term language shift (bilingualism cannot be seen as a guarantee of the survival of a language threatened with decline)?

Spain's experience with democracy and decentralisation, which in practice has meant implementing its own formula for maintaining a system of checks and balances in political power, and experimenting with an original model for institutional diversity (in the form of a new version of federalism), has been relatively brief. It seems that, whereas the principle of pluralism, including linguistic pluralism, has been welcomed nationally in theory, the ways this principle has been implemented (for example, with regard to cultural policies) show that *real* linguistic pluralism, which implies an acceptance of linguistic diversity and all that it entails, has not been fully taken on board. But of course I am prepared to concede that I, as a linguist, may well be much more enthusiastic about linguistic diversity and cultural pluralism than those who take political decisions and those who have to live with the consequences.

References

Alonso Montero, X. (1973) *Informe Dramático Sobre la Lengua Gallega*. Madrid: Akal.
— (1991) *Informe Sobre a Lingua Galega*. Vilaboa (Pontevedra): Edicións do Cumio.
Alvar, M *et al.* (1986) *Lenguas Peninsulares y Proyección Hispánica*. Madrid: Fundación Friedrich Ebert-Instituto de Cooperación Iberoamericana.
Aracil, L.V. (1973) Bilingualism as a myth. *Revista Interamericana Review* 2 (4), 521–33.
Ayala, F. (1991) Defensa y abandono del idioma. *El País* 11 April 1991.
Badía i Margarit, A.M. (1987) El difícil diálogo de las lenguas. *Saber Leer* No. 7, Agosto–Septiembre 1987.
Cambios en la Ley de Normalización Lingüística. *El País* 10 November 1993.
Collins, R. (1990) *The Basques*. Oxford: Basil Blackwell.
Cobarrubias, J. and Garmendia Lasa, C. (1987) Language policy and language planning efforts in Spain. *Proceedings of the International Colloquium on Language Planning*, 25–9 May 1986. International Centre for Research on Bilingualism, Quèbec: Les Presses de l'Université Laval, 144–91.
Comet i Codina, R. (1990) Minority languages in Spain. In D. Gorter *et al.* (eds): *Proceedings of the Fourth International Conference on Minority Languages* Vol. 2 (Western and Eastern European Papers) (pp. 103–13). Clevedon: Multilingual Matters.
Constitución Española (1979). Madrid: Boletín Oficial del Estado.
El Ciervo (Various authors) (Sept–Oct 1987) Las mil caras del bilingüismo: Encuesta de opinión pública y expresión de opiniones, Barcelona.
España 94 (1994) Secretaría General del Portavoz del Gobierno, Ministerio de la Presidencia, Madrid.
Fishman, J. (1991) *Reversing Language Shift*. Clevedon: Multilingual Matters.
Gómez Pin, V. (1994) La dignidad de España. *El País* 18 November 1994.
Goytisolo, J. (1966) [1976] *Señas de Identidad*. Barcelona: Seix Barral.
Green, J.N. (1993) Representations of Romance: Contact, bilingualism and diglossia. In R. Posner and J.N. Green (eds) *Trends in Romance Linguistics and Philology* (Bilingualism and Linguistic Conflict in Romance Vol. 5) (pp. 3–40. Berlin: Mouton de Gruyter.
— (1994) Language status and political aspirations: The case of northern Spain. In M.M. Parry *et al.* (eds) *The Changing Voices of Europe*. Cardiff: University of Wales Press, 155–72.
Hoffmann, C (1988) Linguistic normalisation in Catalonia: Catalan for the Catalans or Catalan for Catalonia? In J.N. Jorgensen *et al.* (eds) *Bilingualism in Society and School*

(Copenhagen Studies in Bilingualism Vol. 5) (pp. 33–44). Clevedon: Multilingual Matters.

— (1991) *An Introduction to Bilingualism*. London: Longman.

Hooper, J (1995) *The New Spaniards*. Harmondsworth: Penguin Books.

Ille, K. (1988) Sprachkonflict im heutigen Spanien: Catalonia, Galicia, Euskadi und Val d'Aran im Vergleich. *Grazer Linguistische Studien* 29 (Spring), 23–34.

Lexislación Actualizada Sobre a Lingua Galega (1989) Consellería de Educación, Xunta de Galicia, Santiago de Compostela.

Ley de Normalización del Uso del Euskera (1986) Bilbao: Servicio de Publicidad, Gobierno Vasco.

Ley de Normalización Lingüística en Cataluña (1983) Departament de Cultura de la Generalitat de Catalunya, Tortosa.

Mar-Molinero, C. (1990) Language policies in post-Franco Spain: Conflict of central goals and local objectives. In R. Clark *et al.* (eds) *Language and Power (British Studies in Applied Linguistics* 5) (pp. 52–63). London: CILT.

Mar-Molinero, C. & Stevenson, P. (1991) Language, geography and politics: The 'Territorial Imperative' debate in the European context. *Language Problems and Language Planning* 15 (2), 162–76.

Mey, J. (1989) 'Saying it don't make it so': The '*Una Grande Libre*' of language politics. *Multilingua* 8 (4), 333–55.

Monteagudo, H. and Santamarina, A. (1993) Galician and Castilian in contact: Historical, social and linguistic aspects. In R. Posner and J.N. Green (eds) *Trends in Romance Linguistics and Philology (Bilingualism and Linguistic Conflict in Romance* Vol. 5) (pp. 117–208). Berlin: Mouton de Gruyter.

Ninyoles, R.L. (1972) *Idioma y Poder Social*. Madrid: Tecnos.

Olmos, E. (1994) ¿Qué es sentirse español? *El País* 4 November 1994.

Paniagua Fuentes, X. (1991) Las reacciones ante el bilingüismo. *Revista de Educación* 262, 103–09.

Rojo, G. (1982) La situación lingüística gallega. *Revista de Occidente* 10–11, 93–110.

Salvador, G. (1983) Sobre la deslealtad lingüística. *Lingüística Española Actual* 5, 174 ff.

— (1987) *Lengua Española y Lenguas de España*. Madrid: Ariel.

Sevilla, F.J. (1986) Algunos aspectos y problemas del multilingüismo. In Manuel Alvar (ed.) *Lenguas Peninsulares y Proyección Hispánica*. Madrid: Fundación Friedrich Ebert & Instituto de Cooperación Iberoamericana.

Siguán, M. (1992) *España Plurilingüe*. Madrid: Alianza Editorial.

Strubell i Trueba, M. (1993) Catalan: Castilia. In R. Posner and J.N. Green (eds) *Trends in Romance Linguistics and Philology (Bilingualism and Linguistic Conflict* Vol. 5) (pp. 175–207). Berlin: Mouton de Gruyter.

Torres, J. (1984) Problems of linguistic normalization in the Països Catalans: From the Congress of Catalan Culture to the present day. *International Journal of the Sociology of Language (Catalan Sociolinguistics)* (pp. 59–62. Amsterdam: Mouton de Gruyter.

Tovar, A. (1982) Bilingüismo en España. *Revista de Occidente* 10–11, 13ff.

Tusón, J. (1988) Señas de identidad. *El País* 30 December 1988

Vallverdú, F (1979) *La Normalitzatió a Catalunya*. Barcelona: Laia.

— (1981) *Conflicto Lingüístico en Cataluña: Historia y Presente*. Barcelona: Península.

Wardhaugh, R. (1987) *Languages in Competition*. Oxford: Blackwell.

Willis, C. (1992) Castilian's Hispanic rivals. *Vida Hispánica* 5, 5–11.

Woolard, K. (1989) *Double Talk: Bilingualism and the Politics of Ethnicity in Catalonia*. Stanford: Stanford University Press.

The Debate

Language Censuses, Planning and Policy

Dennis Ager (Aston University): What I find fascinating about the present situation in Spain is the way that everyone is interested in language and talks about it. In Britain, language is always there and never noticed. In France, the concerns focus on just the one issue — defending French against English.

Charlotte Hoffmann (Salford University): I suppose it is because so much has happened in language planning in Spain. People do talk about language and get very heated; there are articles about it in the press. It has escaped the confines of the academic discipline. You could almost say that Catalonia has become the European centre for Sociolinguistics, perhaps because the area is so well funded by the Catalan government. There is some groundbreaking theoretical work going on there — as well as the essential basics — terminology etc.

Dennis Ager: Can I ask for a definition of planning and policy before we launch into the debate? Planning for me is individuals doing their own thing, choosing their own identity, organising on a local scale. Picking one thing or another, they plan as individuals. And then on the other side you get policy, which is the government telling you what to do or some political organisation which imposes its own views from the top. And that may or may not reflect individual planning. Is there a mismatch here which is worth investigating in the Spanish context?

Charlotte Hoffmann: I have a different definition. I see policy as government-dictated and planning as the implementation of specific measures at a more local/regional level. In each of the three Autonomies there has been some mismatch between these two levels.

Dennis Ager: I suppose, too, that we have to be really careful in this situation; there are so many subtexts, so much activism that is mixed in with the scholarship.

Charlotte Hoffmann: Yes, this is a real problem. The Catalan sociolinguists have been accused of being very 'enthusiastic'. That is why counting speakers gives so many different figures. The difficulties are obvious. In the recent 1990 government survey speakers were asked to say whether they spoke a language 'well'. This is obviously open to interpretation. What does it mean when someone claims to speak a language well? What they are claiming unambiguously is membership of a linguistic group. When the area is so heavily politicised, we have to be very cautious in interpreting the statistics. That is why I've been reluctant to use very many in this paper.

Rafael Sala (Bradford University): We're also working in an area where languages are part of a continuum. For instance, if a census asks if you can understand Galician, then almost all Spanish speakers can answer yes. Whether they do or not depends on their desire to be seen as part of that group — a non-Galician will understand or not, depending on his attitudes rather than on linguistic criteria.

Charlotte Hoffmann: Figures from censuses are notoriously difficult to work with in the best circumstances. They don't give the full picture, they don't say whether the subjects use Galician all the time, have any difficulty with it or if they ever codeswitch to Castilian. School statistics are more useful. We have real data when we know how many pupils have passed examinations in that language, how many teachers using that language have been observed by inspectors, how much teaching material has been produced.

Zsófia Radnai (Pécs University): When you are interpreting claims about language use or language competence, it is always essential to know where and how the data were collected. There is some very interesting work by Peter Nelde which shows that using data collectors with different mother tongues produces different results. Apparently, many people claim language adherence in order to flatter the information gatherer. When this is entangled with linguistic national-ism, it's quite a minefield for objective surveys.

Sue Wright (Aston University): You could describe what is happening in late twentieth century Spain as a continuation of the nineteenth century struggle for the congruence of the political and cultural unit. The Catalans and the Galicians are being mobilised along linguistic lines, aren't they? In the classic tradition of linguistic nationalism. This makes all language census work more a test of allegiance than of patterns of language use and levels of linguistic competence.

Bilingualism and Monolingualism

Charlotte Hoffmann: The other point that we should remember when we discuss language planning is the overwhelming distrust of and dislike for bilingualism in Spain. This may influence people's claims. First of all we have the traditional opinion of Madrid that Spain was a monolingual state and portrayed itself as such to the outside world — like most Western European countries. The basic assumption was that one language would unite the people and keep the state strong. Psychologists and educators backed the politicians — bilingualism was seen as 'harmful' both for the individual and for society. A lot of Castilian speakers would like this still to be the case.

Then we have the Catalans, who fear that Catalan won't survive unless it is the sole language — so there is pressure to use Catalan more and more in public life to oust Castilian. I think the fundamental question in the Catalan situation is whether it is preferable to have societal bilingualism and risk the death of Catalan, or to bear the acrimony from the rest of Spain and to opt for monolingualism and the safeguarding of Catalan. As a linguist I am drawn to bilingualism rather than monolingualism, but the argument is always that bilingualism does not safeguard the less prestigious, i.e. the minority, language.

Alan Yates (Sheffield University): Something needs to be said about the political complications. We cannot forget the particular political context in Spain at present — a precarious socialist-centralist minority held in power by a conservative-nationalist Catalan autonomous government in a country (Spain) where anti-Catalan feeling is widespread and can be whipped up on demand. This has had much to do with the acrimony, with the vehemence and instrumentalisation of the language and identity debate.

There is an orthodoxy in the Catalan language policy which you bring out in your paper; the hidden agenda of the bilingual focusing of normalisation, which is an understanding that bilingualism is a precarious and transitory stage — it can't last — it will resolve itself in extinction of one or other language.

Sue Wright: This is because there aren't clear domains — Catalan is used in all domains for all functions. That is bound to resolve itself in language shift. As Suzanne Romaine has said, if a language doesn't have a clear — and differentiated — role, it will disappear.

Charlotte Hoffmann: But a diglossic situation wouldn't be tolerated. Diglossia is always seen in Spain in terms of conflict between the high and the low varieties. There is a very strong feeling that the lack of prestige of Catalan, Galician etc., stems from their diglossic relationship with Castilian. This is what makes societal bilingualism so hard to achieve in the three Autonomies. In Catalonia there is a feeling that the new law is the only guarantee for the survival of the Catalan language; there is still a lot of doubt whether the language will survive in the long term because of the large numbers of so-called 'immigrants', who have not been Catalanised as quickly as it was envisaged.

Dennis Ager: The language issue is always presented as a problem, but we should really examine whether it is a problem, a right or a resource. If it is a problem, it will be resolved in some way, some solution — monolingualism, bilingualism, managed multilingualism or a mosaic of communities — will be found. If it is a right, then we have to define right — is it the right of the society or of the individual? If it is a resource, then how do we ensure that everyone, the whole society, benefits? In this area, we too often make a basic assumption that the linguistic issue is a *problem*. The Catalan language planning model assumes that the linguistic situation in Catalonia is a problem with only one solution — societal monolingualism in Catalan. Obviously there are a whole range of other solutions possible, and these are being neglected.

Charlotte Hoffmann: That analysis is exactly right. And it has to be said, too, that the model doesn't look further than the immediate 'problem'. Very soon other 'problems' emerge as others demand their rights — for example, the rights of Castilian speakers to use their language on Spanish soil.

Keith Watson (Reading University): If we pursue Dennis' line and look more closely at rights and resources, then the debate becomes very complex. If Catalan is the medium of instruction in the schools and the official language in the public arena, the value of Castilian is reduced. It is the right of the Spanish citizen to have access to the language so that s/he can be a full member of the Spanish state. It is, however, conceivable that this will not be a resource that is valued by every Catalan. As you mention in the paper — how many Catalans would like the right to have English as a second language in the schools to have access to global culture, the global community? Or French to have access to the North? This would mean that they were delinking themselves from the Spanish state in an almost irreversible way. Is this likely to happen?

Charlotte Hoffmann: No. I don't think so at the present moment, because they have contact with Spanish and the rest of Spain all the time and a right and a duty to learn Spanish. Theoretically, it might arise in the future, but the nation state is still very strong.

Keith Watson: If we draw parallels with a part of the world I know well — Singapore — then we see what can happen to a bilingual system. In Singapore the government set up an education system which used four languages as the means of instruction and which had English as the second language. Now the situation has evolved so far that the education system — past a certain age and level — is largely through English. This has been for a variety of reasons — mostly economic and instrumental. The autochthonous languages are preserved at the community level — but there is a danger that English use may spill over in that domain too. In some ways, Singapore is an English-speaking city state.

Rafael Sala: I cannot envisage that Catalonians will ever see anything but Spanish as their link with the wider world. English may well be the most widely-taught foreign language — but it remains just that, a foreign language.

Keith Watson: Yes, I was just pointing out the economic pull of a language like English.

Rafael Sala: But the Spanish will always see Spanish as their link with the wider world — links with South America are very strong. It's an area with immense potential for Spain.

Language and Education

Keith Watson: There is a tension through all this — a pendulum swing from a very strong centralised state which used one language as the educational medium towards a separation where different language media are allowed. This is still resolvable for the nation state if there is a common curriculum which threads through and, therefore, in one sense, it doesn't matter what language it is being delivered in. But if the Catalans then say we are going to teach in Catalan, we are going to develop Catalan literature, develop a separate Catalan curriculum and remove ourselves from the Spanish mainstream, then I foresee problems for Spanish identity in its traditional form. There will be fracturing.

Charlotte Hoffmann: This presupposes that education is the most important element in a person's upbringing — in linguistic or even more general terms. I don't believe this is so. If it were, Welsh-medium education would have had more of an effect. There are an enormous number of Castilian influences in Catalonia — the media, movement of people — none of this is likely to decrease. The work environment is Castilian rather than Catalan.

Bryan Cowan (Reading University): If we just think of the number of hours a child watches television compared to the number of hours they are in class. The influence becomes comparable — and if influence tips one way I would suggest it is to the media.

Sharon Imtiaz (Warwick University): The linguistic problems in education must stem in part from an education system organised at national level and the existence of regional languages used as media of instruction. How often is it the case that teachers trained through Castilian, and with Castilian as their preferred language, find themselves in a situation where they must teach through a language they have mastered less well — or may be teaching through Castilian and not have enough mastery of Catalan, Gallego or Basque to provide bilingual support in the other language? How far is this a problem?

Charlotte Hoffmann: With the new generation, this is less and less an issue and there has been major retraining of older teachers. Catalonia insisted on taking responsibility for teacher training within its own boundaries for this very reason.

Sharon Imtiaz: How much movement is there within Catalonia? Will Aranese speakers be posted outside their area? If I have been trained in Catalonia can I move outside the area?

Charlotte Hoffmann: Yes — all teachers will also have Castilian. It only proves a slight problem when, for example, a non-Basque speaker wants to move to the Basque region. However, the situation is slightly different from Catalonia there: not all Basque schools operate in Basque, and, where they do, it is not necessarily used for all subjects at all times.

Alan Yates: We shouldn't exaggerate this problem. There are problems associated with internal migration but I don't think this is a major one at present. It was certainly a problem in the past, when, in the Franco regime, school teachers who had identified with or supported the Republic were sent to other areas, to Andalusia, for example, as a kind of punishment, and other teachers from areas loyal to the government were drafted into Catalonia to effect a language shift along with a cultural or political shift. There are stories galore of beatings and other punishments used to discourage the speaking of Catalan.

Charlotte Hoffmann: Even today there are still postings to a completely different linguistic area. Teachers have traditionally carried Castilian to all the areas of the state. There is much documentation to show that they often exhibited hostile attitudes towards the local languages they did not speak. It will be a lengthy process getting a whole new cohort of teachers with different attitudes.

Dennis Ager: This is a perennial problem. Language competence is one of the major brakes on internal migration in the European Union. You don't tend to go where you can't operate linguistically, and a sensible system doesn't try to send you.

Srikant Sarangi (University of Wales, Cardiff): This is one of the factors that blocks internal migration in India.

Alan Yates: We ought to point out at some stage that this experiment of language planning, of language policy making, of social engineering, has been remarkably effective and peaceful. It hasn't been perfect but there have been minimal disruptions, embarrassments and inconveniences. It is very significant that even at the height of the protests against Catalanisation there were only 70–80 requests from Castilian-speaking parents to opt out of having their children educated in Catalan. A whole campaign organised by CADECA — a vociferous Castilian support group — only resulted in this meagre number of requests. In all the heat and steam of a very difficult political situation, there was little dissent.

Europe of the Regions

Sue Wright: This point seems to me terribly significant, because looking at it from the outside, not being involved in it as a research area and, therefore, only seeing the broad sweep and missing the intricacies, it does appear — theoretically — as if a delinking process might take place. Catalonia could remove itself from Spain in the long term. At a macro level, the discourse from the European Union is very regionalist and we hear a lot about the Europe of the Regions. At a micro level, the southern French are very enthusiastic about links along the axis Barcelona–Toulouse. For example, the universities cooperate on a number of areas; the chambers of commerce have joint ventures, a lot of funding bids to Brussels come from trans-frontier associations. In this context it seems quite possible that Catalonia would turn northwards, drift north in its associations and alliances.

Alan Yates: I think that the Catalans have been very dynamic in promoting this view and it has been trumpeted by the more triumphalist Catalans as the great opportunity for Catalans. And 'militant' sociolinguists have tried to sell this nexus as the means for a re-Catalanisation of that part of the Languedoc; the more realistic sociolinguists have acknowledged that, when this axis does exist, it speaks Spanish and French, not Catalan.

Sue Wright: But it is not really a language issue. The French who look south do so for good economic reasons. They see the Catalans as their natural partners in a funding bid. The cultural and linguistic similarities are there, but aren't highlighted. Now, if many economic links go north–south and if, at the same time, Catalan–Castilian cultural traditions are weakened by feelings of animosity because of past events and because they are using different languages and therefore have access to different cultures, then it seems quite possible to me that the cohesion of the nation state would be weakened along that border. The fact that the French Catalans are not using the language would perhaps be a minor factor, if the economic links were strong enough.

Alan Yates: You do hear a lot of this kind of talk now. The Catalan politico-linguistic discussion projects itself to the European perspective, imagining a kind of leap-frogging of the nation state. Yes, the activists do look to Europe to give reality to greater Catalonia but I think this is still in the realms of pious hopes — it's a long way off.

Sue Wright: We could argue that if people are talking about it in public fora then cross border identities are *de facto* evolving — however limited this may be.

Rafael Sala: I believe that we are still experiencing the inevitable overreaction, that must take place after 40 years of linguistic repression. The desire to speak only Catalan will go: it's a reaction from the Civil War. I am sure that as the older generations disappear, the passion there has been for reintroducing Catalan, for only speaking Catalan, will be muted. The younger generation will not have the same political reactions — the demand for monolingualism will fade, the call for even more autonomy will wither. People will take a more pragmatic view — economics will be a more important criterion than cultural loyalty.

Dennis Ager: I am sure in this context and for all the reasons you mention, you are right. Reactions will eventually calm. However, the law of the pendulum is that it will always swing the other way. I'm just wondering how far it will go. If we use Wales and Quebec as actual examples of what may happen, we note that language use hasn't waned after the initial euphoria of being able to use the language again in the public sphere. All the documentation on Welsh use shows that it is increasing — whether we look at the schools, the arts, whatever. In the case of Quebec the illustration is even more telling. One can now live as a monolingual French-speaker in Quebec. In every sphere one is catered for in French. It is the English-speaker who feels linguistically constrained. Political autonomy for Quebec is also on the cards. There, things haven't calmed! It does seem possible to me that this scenario could be re-enacted in Catalonia.

Charlotte Hoffmann: I think that this fear certainly exists. All parts of Spain are involved in the debate. People are very anxious. The language debate, the identity debate, the allegiance debate are not just of interest within the Autonomies.

Rafael Sala: I think people are worried too about the extent to which linguistic freedom will go in the country as a whole. How many languages can the Spanish state tolerate? There are now 17 languages which would like to be treated as separate, so that their linguistic communities can benefit from the special treatment that derives from this status. This is clearly not possible. It is like Yorkshire declaring itself to have a separate idiom and then wishing to be treated as separate. I think these linguistic demands must fade or the state will fracture.

Sue Wright: Well I think that was the point we were making before — we can't rule out the fracturing of the nation state in the long term. And as for very similar languages delinking, this is not quite as unlikely as it sounds. There are blueprints for this. Czech and Slovak are linguistically two varieties of the same language. When those with political and economic power wanted the Czechs and Slovaks to be treated as an entity, differences were minimised. When the Slovakian elites were seeking independence, suddenly differences were underlined. The whole thing about language varieties is that if people find it useful for quite other reasons — economic or political — to cease to be part of a whole then the language differences will be stressed.

Nationalism and Language

Dennis Ager: Let's look at the same point from the other end. How strong is the feeling of Spain and Spanish? In Britain the reaction to the possibilities of European federalism, to any suggestion of a Europe of the Regions, has been a nationalist backlash. What about those outside the Autonomies, is there any agitation to try and contain the fracturing, to return to the idea of Spain as the nation state?

Charlotte Hoffmann: What is quite interesting is how nationalism was a fairly late development in Spain. It never caught on in quite the way it did elsewhere — for instance there is a lack of symbols (e.g. squares and monuments) to commemorate the great moments of the past. There was no anthem, no flag until relatively late. Even the imposition of Castilian didn't have a nationalist dimension. The phrase was 'Speak *Christian*'!

Sue Wright: But Catalan nationalism has always been strong, hasn't it? The state has always had to deal with the North East region's rejection of central authority.

Alan Yates: It took off in the nineteenth century as a process of romantic revivalism which became increasingly politicised as the Catalan economy became stronger — or, rather, economic development marked even more strongly the pre-existing differentials between Catalonia and the rest of the Spanish state. So, by the end of the nineteenth century you've got, in very broad brush terms, the politicisation of a sort of eisteddfodish revivalist movement, which during the twentieth century makes positive gains in terms of devolution, self-government, autonomy, institutions, standardisation, codification of language, education, the beginnings of a self-governing, semi-federal — confederal — entity within the Spanish state. And in 1931 this region even has the nerve to declare itself independent, to declare itself the Catalan Republic within the Spanish Republic. The Spanish state rejected that, of course, and the resulting compromise was the Generalitat — the compromise restitution of a medieval political entity.

The point is that it is a rising graph — rising steadily throughout the nineteenth century. At the end of the century Spain lost her colonies. As the Catalans had been doing a lot of business with the empire, there was distinct disgruntlement in Barcelona and a feeling that Madrid wasn't making a very good job of running the show. This fuelled the feeling that they would be better off on their own. So there was a strong surge of Catalan nationalism in 1898, then again in 1901 through to the 1930s. They made spectacular progress in terms of political and linguistic achievement.

After that it is interesting to note what happened during the 40 years of 'repression'. The impact on Catalan society and Catalan language was immense and this explains in part why there is pressure to slough that off. However, in the paper you make the point very strongly that it is perhaps a mistake to apply criteria now that were valued in the 1930s, and I tend to agree with you.

Dennis Ager: How much do the events where Spain was definitely acting as an entity against the outsider, e.g. the Reconquista, act as a potent force in the collective consciousness? Is there collective pride in 'national' endeavours — 1492 for example?

Alan Yates: Well, that is really going back. We could perhaps just look at the Catalans and Madrid in the eighteenth century. There was strong reaction to Bourbon centralism, which caused a lot of perplexity amongst Bourbon centralisers, who came in and said, 'These are funny people these Catalans, they insist on speaking their own language'. All the attractions and the beguilements of the Enlightenment and centralisation, which were considerable in Spain under Charles III, didn't stop the Catalans from continuing to speak their own language — in spite of Madrid's contempt. They were described as having a language which wasn't much use for anything, a dead provincial language that was 'no use to man nor beast', which wasn't 'fit for writing books' — for example we can see this in the *Memorias Históricas* of A. de Capmany (1785). And then by 1833, under the influence of romantic nationalism, you'd got the grammars and the dictionaries and the activists saying 'Pluck down your lyres from the walls, boys, we're going to have a troubadour revival'. In the language of the troubadours — Limousin, Provençal — it didn't really matter. It was the period of Ossian — you had to have a glorious past. That was the beginning of the revival.

The Catalans were lucky in that social cohesion coincided with an industrial revolution which gave them a bourgeoisie with a vested interest in marking off their difference from the plebs who spoke rural Catalan — they, themselves, spoke elevated Catalan — the language of the troubadours and which differentiated them too from the Castilian speakers, who had made such a mess of losing the Empire.

Dennis Ager: You mention grammars and dictionaries. So standardisation and corpus planning were well advanced by the end of the century?

Alan Yates Yes, Catalan has a strong tradition in this. The intellectuals and activists wanted the language to be a common literary language apt for use in all normal everyday situations. And this had been achieved by the 1930s — not just in the principality of Catalonia but it was also agreed for Valencia and the Balearic Islands, which are also Catalan speaking territories with their own administrations and nowadays their own language policies and a whole set of differentiating political and social problems. But that degree of standardisation, codification was achieved in the first 30 years of the century and is not problematic.

Dennis Ager: That I find hard to credit. Standardisation is always problematic. French, for example, has been standardised for a considerable time but it isn't by any means standardised and is always under pressures to change — Quebec, francophone Africa, feminism, the move to the cities. There are all sorts of reasons, all sorts of pressures on the language to evolve. There are incredible tensions all the time.

Alan Yates: Well, of course this is true of Catalan also — I wouldn't want to give the impression that it was fixed in the 1930s in any kind of definitive way. Rather it was a coming together and codifying of varieties. Don't get me wrong — the dictionary is constantly being renewed and the grammars and descriptions adapted.

Dennis Ager: An enormous amount of money is poured into the French operation — terminology banks, legislation, new dictionaries etc. Is the same sort of thing happening in Catalonia?

Charlotte Hoffmann: Very much so. In Catalonia they have really done a great deal, on the one hand modernising and on the other 'purifying' the language — because Catalan and Galician had been Castilianised. There has been a great deal of debate as to which items should be rejected and which adapted. It is an ongoing process. In Galicia there is the added interest that purification often leads to an impasse: there is no word, so where is the new word to come from? From Portuguese, from Castilian?

Sue Wright: Can you talk about revitalisation in connection with Galician? Had the language reached the point where, if something had not been done to promote it, it would have faded away?

Charlotte Hoffmann: Yes, perhaps. People have been writing about the future of Galician in very pessimistic terms for some time, probably because it had come to be used in very reduced functions — certain kinds of work, rural communities and amongst older people. To that extent, yes, we can talk about revitalisation because it was necessary to make the language fit for other purposes.

Sue Wright: Could we go a little deeper into a point you make in the paper? I've understood that the normalisation and codification that are necessary for making Galician fit for use — as an educational medium for example — are actually detaching it from its speakers. If there is an immense effort to put in place a new standard with which the majority of speakers are not familiar, in a sense this replicates the linguistic problems and alienations caused by the distance between Castilian and the Galician dialect. The rural dialect speaker has only changed from being an imprecise user of Castilian to being an imprecise user of Galician — and since this is his/her 'own' language this discrepancy may be felt more keenly than the previous one. We should ask ourselves what the point of revitalisation must be. Is it in part to promote 'continuity' of a language so that its speakers can keep their allegiance to the language, so that they can have access to traditional sources and cultural wealth? If you change it so that many people don't feel that continuity — even if the changes are not great linguistically — does that not call into question the whole process?

Charlotte Hoffmann: Yes — because to some extent it is an artificial process. Promoting a standard that is new to everybody — as was the case in the Basque country where the standard, a new variety based loosely on one of the seven, not mutually comprehensible, varieties of Basque, caused just such problems. And, of course, acceptance is a very lengthy process. It is also a very politicised process in Galicia. There are two camps — one wishes to form closer links with Portugal and one wishes to promote a distinct form which is independent of the surrounding varieties. If the integrationists are winning it is because they are more active, publish more prolifically etc. So the revitalisation of Galician is very complex. It is necessary to get a range of people to accept the standard — those who only spoke Castilian before, those who wanted the other standard, ss well as the rural dialect speakers who may or may not recognise the standard as their language variety. And, in addition, it is not only a question of recovering the language but also of undertaking language spread. It is being introduced into areas where it was not present before. It is remarkable that there has been the success that there has been in the last 20 years.

Helen Kelly-Holmes (Aston University): Certainly language recovery and spread didn't work in the Irish context.

Charlotte Hoffmann: The advances in technology are on the side of the Galicians — communication, media, educational materials development is all much easier to do on a small scale with the new technologies. Revitalisation here does also coincide with other changes in society. We are talking about rural speakers in this context and those rural communities are themselves disappearing with the drift to the towns.

Bryan Cowan (Reading University): But there is tangible evidence of language revitalisation in Galicia. In the last few years, use of Gallego has become much more public and official. The road signs, for example, are now mainly in Gallego and anything left in Castilian attracts graffiti and defacing. And it is not just symbolic use. In the university at Santiago the usual language is now Gallego. My colleagues will speak Castilian to me because I'm a foreigner but few exceptions are made — and that is a very recent development.

The Influence of the Media

Charlotte Hoffmann: It is true that there is this feeling of pride and therefore a willingness to use Gallego. It is significant that it is the university which is doing so! However, the other processes continue. Even those who remain on the land are not linguistically isolated — urban ways of life are spreading out. For example, habitual television watchers are being influenced even when they stay in the country.

Alan Yates: Television is nowadays a very strong force for language standardisation, and here it is playing that role very effectively.

Charlotte Hoffmann: Except, perhaps, that programmes in the regional languages are generally rated as boring. The average Catalan viewer — the Basque, the Galician — tends to assess regionally controlled television as more worthy, but less glamorous, less attractive than national television which is in Castilian!

Alan Yates: This is one of the ways in which the Basques and Galicians could have learnt from the Catalans' mistakes.

Mike Grover (Multilingual Matters): But it comes down to money really. Do regional television companies have the resources to finance lavish, exciting, glamorous productions?

Charlotte Hoffmann: Well, no. But it isn't only that. There is an earnestness and worthiness about regional TV. The idealists are out to improve the viewers rather than entertain — with all the obvious consequences.

Bryan Cowan: The Galicians have made a great effort to appeal to the younger members of their audience. There are quiz shows which have upper age limits — only under-30s are allowed to attend. This has been very popular.

Charlotte Hoffmann: This group is, of course, the group which feels most at home in the new norm. They are the ones who will perhaps have had some education in the language.

Christina Schäffner (Aston University): When a series is bought from foreign producers, is it dubbed into Castilian or into the regional languages?

Alan Yates: This is a very interesting point — I would say that the fact that Catalan TV bought *Dallas* and dubbed it into Catalan had as much impact on changing language use as any educational policy.

Christina Schäffner: Was it also dubbed into Castilian and was this version watched in preference to the Catalan version in the country?

Alan Yates: No — people watched it in Catalan — even in strong Castilian ghettos. It had tremendous influence. Catalonia has a good reputation for skilful dubbing and subtitling.

Bryan Cowan: They also bought *Eastenders* and copied it. *Poble Nou* is an obvious copy of *Eastenders*, set in the cheap end of Barcelona, down by the port. It shows aspects of Barcelona life, together with all the topics and clichés of soap opera melodrama.

Sharon Imtiaz: Presumably a native soap opera has a symbolic effect. Catalans see it as reflecting back 'our culture to us in our own language'. It is much more than the sum of its parts, much more than just a soap opera in Catalan. It legitimises an identity.

Alan Yates: Yes. Its influence on the autochthonous population in Barcelona has been enormous and we shouldn't forget what effect it will have on allochthonous groups. Catalonia has been an economic magnet and Barcelona is now home to a very heterogeneous population. *Poble Nou* promotes Catalan identity amongst both groups.

Srikant Sarangi: This is very typical of post-modern identity — there is the pull of global identity but to access it we have to go through layers of local identity. There is *Dallas* and *Eastenders* but also the local home-grown soap opera which gives us terms of reference, familiarity, accessibility. So here we have not just multiple identities but multiple fragmented identities.

Alan Yates: Perhaps better categorised as transactional identities. I think we have to be cautious here because this process is as much a part of the modernising process in Catalonia as a part of the Catalan post-modernist discourse. As the turn-of-the-century *modernista* poet, Maragall, the grandfather of the present mayor of Barcelona, said, for true universalism you have to dig your feet deeper into tradition.

Dennis Ager: It depends what sort of identity you are talking about. In the case of *Dallas* and its dubbing into Catalan, I'm not sure I see how the language plays a part in reinforcing Catalan identity. Surely the television viewer watching *Dallas* is accessing American culture — global culture in a sense — and the medium is the language he understands? I don't imagine the medium has much weight compared to the message.

Srikant Sarangi: No, the two are juxtaposed. They may, if they do not fit, cause an identity crisis.

Identities

Sharon Imtiaz: I'd like to come back to the the point made by Sue earlier about the Catalan identity negating the Spanish nation state identity. It seems to me that in Catalonia, at this juncture, structuring of identities is likely to happen in a way that could bypass the modern state. There is no reason why you can't have a leap in this particular instance from the local/regional to Europe — or to the US. The one place influence is not coming from appears to be Madrid.

Sue Wright: Catalonia does seem to be a place to watch to see if power is leaking upwards and downwards, as we are constantly told that it will. On the question of identities, it would be interesting to know whether in a situation of flux and change any of the groups in the equation are saying: yes belong to us, but we discourage you from belonging to any or some of the others. Are new kinds of exclusive fraternities evolving in Catalonia?

Srikant Sarangi: This will take you beyond language identities.

Sue Wright: A language identity is only part of a greater whole. An identity is composed of several elements and language may be one of them.

Charlotte Hoffmann: Leaving out the identities deriving from family and just looking at group identities, in the Iberian peninsula they have the following identities: local identity, regional identity, national identity, Spanish, Iberian peoples, the Mediterranean identity, the European Union identity. Some may be stronger than others but they are likely to be present in some sense.

Sue Wright: Wouldn't any problem with such a multiple identity come from the outside? There is only conflict when one of the groups to which you feel you belong says you can only have our identity and no other. Layers of identity are psychologically unproblematic if no-one is forcing you to shed one or telling you that multiple identities are impossible. And it's usually the nation state which pushes for exclusivity. There are ways of pressurising, for example, economic punishment — you won't be able to progress up your career ladder unless you adopt the dominant language. Is the region pushing for exclusivity in the same way?

Srikant Sarangi: Well, almost unquestionably. We're assuming that we select our identities, that we have a choice of multiple identities. We ought to recognise too that a kind of identity is imposed on us — by authority, the politicians, the government.

Alan Yates: I've been thinking that there are layers of contradiction, of confusion here, particularly when we move out into generalisations which move us into the danger of national stereotypes. I think there's a way of addressing this slightly differently, not turning it inside out but instead looking at the formula that was used by the language planners and politicians together. The definition of a Catalan for these people was s/he who lives and works in Catalonia. So this is a very territorial type of definition. It skirts by the autochthonous/allochthonous and it overcomes the difficulties of the individual/collective dichotomy. You don't need to choose.

Srikant Sarangi: Exactly! The authorities define what group identity is to a large extent, impose an identity, impose a language.

Alan Yates: It's interesting that you see it as imposition, because it wasn't offered as an imposition. It was an olive branch. The message to those living on Catalan soil was, 'Don't worry if you are here, you are part of us. Don't worry that you don't speak Catalan yet, so long as you are happy here and you are working here, you are Catalan.'

Srikant Sarangi: Surely that's an imposition? It may have been marketed as a good thing, but it's basically an imposition.

Charlotte Hoffmann: Once you take the decision in favour of the territoriality principle then everything else follows from that. Once you pass legislation that says Catalan is the language of this autonomy, then you are committed — policies are fixed and people are obliged to carry them out.

Dennis Ager: You will agree that there has been imposition? You have to take it or leave it.

Srikant Sarangi: It's not a question of take it or leave it. Once it has been decreed you must take it — that's what I mean by imposition.

Dennis Ager: That's a little simplistic. History and recent history is full of examples where people haven't 'taken' it. The whole of Eastern Europe is a case in point.

Sue Wright: But that's a false parallel. The parallel is much more with a place like France, where boundaries were established early on and the territorial principle accepted from, arguably, the Revolution. Once you are within those boundaries you are French, and if you're not French, don't worry, our education system will make you so. That is more or less what Charlotte seems to be saying — don't worry, if you're not Catalan, we'll 'Catalanise' you.

Alan Yates: That's a caricature.

Sue Wright: But here, perhaps, the caricature has a grain of truth in it. The territorial principle is inclusive, but it also stamps out difference. It is a complete rejection of diversity.

Alan Yates: But in this instance we must remember that the territorial principle also extends to the Spanish state. And the issue is complicated by the relationship between the state and the Autonomy. You don't have that complication in the French situation.

Sue Wright: No, here you have another layer to which you have recourse. What would happen if you were living in Catalonia, were not Catalan speaking, and wished to have a career in the public sphere — not in any family business or small private concern? Is it not true that you would have to acquire Catalan, you would have to Catalanise yourself?

Alan Yates: That is one way of defining in practical terms the implications of normalisation and it's understood to be the recovery of a position towards which Catalonia was heading when it was illegitimately interrupted by the uprising in 1936. The constitution of 1979, the statute of autonomy and the language law of 1983 pick up provisions established and laws passed in the 1930s.

Rafael Sala: I wonder how much truth there is in this idea of multiple identities. I've been in Britain for 21 years and yet I haven't taken British citizenship. I can't help being Catalan (not in any nationalistic sense, I'd like to stress) even though I speak Castilian and English. I have no desire to take on multiple identities with my multilingualism.

Economics

Keith Watson: I've been thinking of our last debate when John Edwards talked about the Quebec situation. We felt then that the whole question of identity was linked closely to economic advantage, i.e. you work here, you live here, it would pay you to join us identificationally and linguistically.

Rafael Sala: I believe it is almost impossible to separate the economic factor from everything else. In purely economic terms, there is no doubt that you do not need all these languages, Basque, Catalan, Galician. For example, a book about reinforced concrete is difficult enough to sell in Spanish, never mind in Catalan or Basque. But, during the transition, the Spanish prime minister asserted that Catalan was not a suitable language for talking about nuclear physics and immediately every Catalan scientist set out to prove him wrong, showed him that works did exist already in Catalan, that science should be published in Catalan. But who pays to replace the books, when we can in fact get the information through Castilian? At the end of the day, the sheer economic advantage of Spanish is going to be a major factor.

Dennis Ager: If I summarise what we've just said, we are almost coming to the conclusion that language is of secondary or even tertiary importance in terms of identification. In this case geographical considerations — just being on the territory — are key because they give you your appellation. Then, economic advantage influences you to buy into the territorially imposed identity. And language and, presumably, culture are just further elements in your decision-making, if indeed you do have a choice.

Alan Yates: History is also a major factor.

Dennis Ager: If we keep on the economic argument for a moment or two, we can see why two of the three Autonomies might attract people to them. Barcelona is an economic magnet, so were the Asturias.

Charlotte Hoffmann: These are industrial centres. There is nothing in Galicia or the Basque country which has the cultural significance or prestige of Barcelona.

Alan Yates: The structure of Basque society and the structure of Galician society are quite different from the structure of Catalan society. Catalan has gone through the classic bourgeois liberal industrial and post-industrial evolution — even to the extent that you have got this great capital, with its hinterland and the normal tensions that this situation brings.

Rafael Sala: This caused different patterns of identification. The great Basque bourgeois families were Castilian speaking — even at the end of the nineteenth century, whereas that was not the case in Catalonia.

Charlotte Hoffmann: This is true. In the Basque country any would-be member of the middle classes would not speak Basque because of the stigma attached to it and because it was seen to be so closely related to ETA. Even parties with moderate regionalist agendas decided not to speak Basque. Then splinter groups close to ETA made language a rallying point and politicised the issue. Now there is growing middle class support — on a small scale — for Basque since this ETA association has weakened.

Srikant Sarangi: If we think of economics rather than the perspective of the individual, then language can be treated as a commodity which doesn't have an intrinsic value of its own. Languages are given value by the context, by the market. This is what we must have in mind and explore when we discuss the nineteenth century Catalans who spoke Catalan and the nineteenth century Basques who spoke Castilian. In the context of Catalonia, because you have wealthy people in a wealthy society speaking the language, then this language has prestige. In another context where the relatively more successful in a poorer society opt to use the language of an outside group then the autochthonous — majority — language assumes the characteristics of a disfavoured minority language.

Rafael Sala: Exactly. The confident, rich Catalans have always been very proud to speak their language in public. The poor, uneducated Galicians have been ashamed. In the case of the Basques, speaking in general, attitudes are irrelevant because the people with power and money who would have monopolised the public arena have spoken Castilian.

Alan Yates: While proclaiming themselves Basque.

Rafael Sala: Yes, of course. The Basque bourgeoisie always identified with its ethnic group regardless of language use.

Centre and Periphery

Sue Wright: We've looked at Madrid imposing the Castilian language and cultural norms from the centre. Was this accompanied by clear prejudice, clear expressions of perceived superiority? In the French context there are some wonderful examples of racist discourse about Southerners — and from very well-known and respected figures — Stendhal, Taine, Mérimée.

Alan Yates: During the nineteenth century, the relative weakness of Madrid as a capital meant that feelings of superiority did not really feature. The contempt of the centre for the periphery is very much a feature of the Fascist period. In the nineteenth century, I feel it would be fair to speak of the respect of Madrid for Barcelona and the Basque country because of their mercantile, commercial and industrial prowess.

Charlotte Hoffmann: Well yes. But we mustn't forget that there is also the legacy of a long history of struggle between the periphery and the centre. We can note the continuing strength of feeling, perhaps from the demands that are made about terminology. For instance, the Catalans totally reject the term 'minority language'. They won't tolerate Madrid terming them a minority; they always quote their 6,000,000 speakers as being significant in European terms and they have made it quite clear in their various attempts within the EU that they want their language to be a working language of the EU.

Alan Yates: We mustn't forget that each of the areas, Galicia, the Basque country and Catalonia all have very different experiences and it would be wrong to treat them as a whole. The Basque and Galician relationship with Madrid has been very different from the Catalan one.

The Northern Catalans

Sue Wright: When you come across the border into Northern Catalonia, into France, the language has been diluted quite a bit by the French education system. Do the people there still have a distinct Catalan identity?

Rafael Sala: My feeling is that, apart from the activists, most people look in the direction of Paris, whether they speak Catalan or not. This is particularly true for the young people.

Alan Yates: Yes. Paris is the magnet rather than Barcelona, even though Barcelona is a much more accessible capital for them. It is clear that, despite the vigour of Catalan south of the Pyrennees, and despite the pious hopes of the pan-Catalanists and the articulateness of the Catalan activists, Catalan north of the border is dying on its feet. When you are in the country you can see and hear this, it is quite clear. That doesn't mean that all tokens of identity have disappeared from Northern Catalonia; they're very keen on the 'kilt and bagpipe' aspect of identity, as it were. At the same time, they refuse to speak Catalan to their children or grandchildren.

Sue Wright: French propaganda against regional languages has been remarkably successful. Once you have been through the French education system, which is designed to promote national cohesion and identity, you have to be very determined to continue using the regional language and refusing the national language.

Alan Yates: The subtext of what you're saying is that French centralism has been much more effective than Spanish centralism. And the role of the Church is not to be underestimated in Spain. The church was crucial in that the regional language was retained there and people associated in that language, in that context — this supplied continuity and a basis for subsequent social normalisation of the language.

Sue Wright: Of course, in the South of France there was a very strong Protestant presence early on which taught the bible through French, but then of course that faded after the Révocation de l'Edit de Nantes.

Immigration and Regional Revivalism

Sharon Imtiaz: A preoccupation with regionalism usually means that immigrant groups fair badly. Is this true in Spain? Is there any space for multicultural education or language maintenance amongst the Moroccan minorities, for example?

Bryan Cowan: No. You're absolutely right. I would say quite unequivocally that regionalism is limiting the development of immigrant education in Spain. There is no 'celebration of cultural diversity' in any of the three areas we've examined. There is, however, an awareness of this and some groups are posing problems in educational terms. So, just recently, there has been a lot of discussion about multicultural education, intercultural education. There have been a number of meetings and conferences on the subject in the mid-1990s. In many ways, the situation replicates that in Britain in the 1970s. There is the same perception on the part of the ethnic Spanish that there are far more immigrants than there actually are. There is an exaggerated fear about illegal immigration. In general, all the discussion has a negative tinge. The celebration of diversity is not yet an idea that resonates in the Spanish context.

Keith Watson: I wonder if there is actually much celebrating of diversity anywhere. Our comments on this ought to be set in the context of the backlash against multiculturalism throughout the Western World. Just to cite a few things: the reaffirming of English as the language of the community in America, the code of nationality in France, the retrenchment in Britain. I don't see any kind of celebration of diversity anywhere in Europe. So why would Spain be different — particularly since the Spaniards are perhaps not as involved as some of the northern European countries? Is the lack of attention to multiculturalism an anti-immigrant stance? Or is it just the great pleasure of a newly emergent region able at last to celebrate it own identity, but neglecting to make space for newcomers?

Alan Yates: We should remember, too, that Catalan has been recognised and has established itself in the same kind of time span as the move towards recognising the rights of allochthonous groups and the elaboration of theories of multi-culturalism. The Catalans were very concerned to be seen to be squeaky clean about Aranese — they didn't want to be seen to be perpetuating the discrimina-tory policies they themselves had suffered

Bryan Cowan: In addition, the perception of the Spaniards is that immigration is young, male and transient. This is not true — or not wholly true — but it does have an effect on policy-making in general and on multiculturalism in education in particular. There is still a tendency for immigrant groups to keep a low profile, to attempt to be invisible.

Sharon Imtiaz: We are speaking as if the Spaniards are out of line. Sweden apart, there is not a great deal of multiculturalism explicitly promoted as part of European national education systems.

Bryan Cowan: Indeed. The references to it in our own National Curriculum are faint.

And Finally

Rafael Sala: There are so many people who say that it is impossible to think of a Catalonia without Catalan. Yet I must say, as a bilingual, as a linguist, as a Catalan, as someone who is totally convinced that a monolingual cannot grasp what it means to be bilingual, I'm still not persuaded that there cannot be a Catalonia without Catalan. In so many instances we can see the separation of linguistic identity and cultural identity. For practical purposes, Scots Gaelic and Irish have gone and all or most of the Scots and Irish are monolingual English speakers, and yet it seems very clear that the Scots and Irish have a very clear and separate identity. Catalan identity could be expressed through Castilian.

Charlotte Hoffmann: What I find interesting is that in all these discussions of language and identity the emphasis has been on group. As a bilingual — or multilingual — myself, I resent this instruction to take on identities because I am part of a speech community. Certainly I feel neither exclusively one thing nor the other. Would a more bilingual world cause a change in this constricted way of thinking?